T0193107

Also, by
Jacqueline Pridgen Howard

Angels
An Intro to Angels (workbook)
Moving On With Coaching: Daily Journal
Happy Mind Matrix (Co-Author)

Interested in the following services:
Keynote Speaker
Workshop Leader
Or, Coaching Services
Contact me via email for available dates and rates
movingonwithcoaching@gmail.com
or
www.movingonwithcoaching.com

LEADING
GOD'S WAY

JACQUELINE PRIDGEN HOWARD

authorHOUSE®

AuthorHouse™
1663 Liberty Drive
Bloomington, IN 47403
www.authorhouse.com
Phone: 1 (800) 839-8640

Published by AuthorHouse 07/24/2019

ISBN: 978-1-7283-0449-6 (sc)
ISBN: 978-1-7283-0448-9 (hc)
ISBN: 978-1-7283-0447-2 (e)

Library of Congress Control Number: 2019903202

Print information available on the last page.

CONTENTS

FOREWORD

It is with great honor and immeasurable joy that I've been afforded the opportunity to pen these words of encouragement to the author, as well as words of exaltation and affirmation to the reader of this precious book. As a Pastor for more than 35 years, I've discovered that a leader is who you are, and leadership is what you do. I've also come to learn that long after you've gone, a person remembers more of what you've done than what you have said. That is to say; leadership is an action and not just words. I've come to know this woman as such. A person of action and not just words.

I am honored to be a spiritual father, the Pastor, of Elder Dr. Jacqueline Howard for over 33 years. We have witnessed the hand of the Lord upon her as He visibly defines and molds her into her divine destiny, in which this book is. Jeremiah 29:11 says; "For I know the plans that I have for you,' declares the LORD, 'plans for well-being, and not for calamity, in order to give you a future and a hope." It is clear that she is operating in the plans that God have for her. The various ministry work that she has done over the years has clearly defined who she is, and that is; "a leader in the kingdom." A leader is who she is, and leadership is what she so graciously does. This topic Leadership will always be an important topic in our society and even in the church of God. Good leaders nowadays are getting harder to find. This means that any information or resources given to enhance the quality of leadership will be immeasurable in value.

I've discovered that every person is a type of leader. Every person, whether they realize it or not influences someone else. This means that it is crucial that we inform men and women on how to be effective leaders that will better the world. This book provides and accomplishes that goal. It gives directions, and it enlightens the reader concerning the spirit of excellence that will propel them forward to be an inspiring leader. Yes, we need more leaders with the character explained in this book.

I am very proud of Dr. Howard for what she has contributed to the community that she serves and especially to the church. I know from experience that it is much easier to write about something that you know and practice daily. I say to Dr. Howard, continue to push forward. You are not empty yet. Keep writing; we need to hear what you have to say. Jesus said on one occasion; "feed my sheep, feed my lamb." This book is a full course meal that is edible for both the sheep and the lamb. The old and the new. Jesus also said; "the harvest is great, but the labors are few." I need to inform you that you are numbered with the few.

May the lord countenance continue to shine all over you as you continue pursuing your destiny.

Yours truly,

Bishop Varnie Fullwood
President/Founder
North Carolina Theological Seminary

DEDICATION

To Roscoe Howard, my husband

Thank you for demonstrating daily what it means to lead God's way. You have shown me that meekness is not a weakness, but, it is power under control. You always manage to consider the needs of others and consistently show kindness and humility in all that you do. You dependably put God first and somehow never lose sight of the primary objective. I appreciate your willingness to provide instruction, guidance, resources, and your unfailing love. It does not go unnoticed. Thank you so much for nurturing my growth. You are awesome, and I am grateful to be on this journey with you.

To Derek, Monica, and Brielle

You mean more to me than you will ever know. Thank you for always inspiring me, believing in me, and being the best cheer squad ever. You are smart, compassionate, wise, respectful, and possess a sense of humor that simply brightens my day. I am grateful and so very proud to be your mom and Brielle's Nana. May each of you reach the destiny God has planned for you. "I LOVE YOU, FOREVER!"

ACKNOWLEDGEMENTS

Writing a book was never something I thought I would do. Then, in 2010, I wrote my first book, "Angels." After I wrote it, I didn't give writing another book a second thought. I felt as if I was finished, why not? I never aspired to be an author anyway! However, God had other plans for my life, as He often does. He uses others to plant seeds so that they may grow. Several years ago, Darby Scott did just that. She allowed God to speak through her and suggested I write a book on leadership. At the time, I appreciated her confidence in me but could not see it in my future. Today, I dedicate "Leading God's Way" to Darby Scott.

Special thanks are in order to Bishop Varnie N. Fullwood, President and Founder of the North Carolina Theological Seminary, spiritual advisor, mentor, and one who is a constant source of inspiration and guidance. Dr. Janice Brown, editor extraordinaire, thank you for your reassuring confidence and expertise. Chaplain Joyce Boykin, my relentless cheerleader, you will never know how much your love and prayers have meant to me. A special thank you to my friend, Kristi Jernigan who graciously offered to read the roughest of drafts. Thank you for helping me start the editing process.

Above all, I give honor to God who has sustained me through this project and is still keeping me. I am grateful for life, health, abilities, creative insight, and being entrusted with the assignment of helping people grow into whom He has called them to be. I pray that my work helps build stronger communities of self-assured men and women living in alignment with the Word of God. And may it be for HIS Glory.

INTRODUCTION

If you are a follower of Christ and are sincerely seeking to demonstrate His character in your leadership, this book is an excellent resource for your use. It will help you reflect on where you are and where you desire to be. It will also help you in discovering areas of needed improvement while providing you with strategies to aid your growth. If you are not a Christian, the strategies in this book will offer you ways to strengthen the relationships in your organization and hopefully plant seeds for your salvation. According to the Bible, we all have sinned (Romans 3:23) and are separated from God, but, by our faith in God (Ephesians 2:8-9) we can be saved and receive His grace. Romans (10:9-10) states, "If you declare with your mouth, 'Jesus is Lord,' and believe in your heart that God raised Him from the dead, you will be saved." God has made the road to salvation uncomplicated and it is available to all.

Many things will affect one's leadership style, changing circumstances, and people. I believe that no leader strictly adheres to only one leadership style. That would be counter-intuitive in many situations. Regardless of your preferred style, you can, if you choose, incorporate characteristics of Christ in all that you do. You get to decide how much you include. Leadership styles, like personalities, will vary and have many different nuances. They will also have some similarities. However, you will be most comfortable with a style that fits your personality. Your personality will show up in your leadership style; so, embrace it as you allow God to use you to lead others.

The purpose of this book is to elevate leadership one person, one team, and one organization at a time in a manner that reflects the characteristics of Christ. I am convinced that what I offer here will provide valuable insight into effectively leading others. I believe that leaders should pay it forward, be concerned with the development of others, and assist them in reaching their fullest potential. They should take time to mentor other aspiring leaders and endeavor to make a difference in their lives, both personally and professionally. Doing so will prove rewarding to both parties. I believe, coach, and teach servant leadership, a transformative leadership, which creates a culture within organizations that promotes unity. I am here to assist you in "Leading God's Way."

Remember, your leadership sets the tone for how your organization moves forward and establishes or reinforces the organizational CORE VALUES. These principles are the producers of organizational culture. When "Leading God's Way," there is real respect for diversity. Mind you; diversity encompasses more than cultural differences or the hiring of individuals from different backgrounds. It is about building a plan in which everyone believes that they have an equal opportunity to contribute and advance within the organization. As you read this book, keep an open mind and expect to find something in here that resonates with you.

CHAPTER 1

What Is Leadership?

"An empowered life begins with serious personal questions about oneself. Those answers bare the seeds of success."
Steve Maraboli

What makes a leader? According to the article "Portrait of a Leader" by Lashway, Mazzarela, and Grundy, leadership is defined as one occupying a position with formal authority over others that requires vision and is the force that moves others to accomplish a task. Bernard Bass noted that there is a reasonably high correlation between intelligence and leadership ability. The implication is that having a mastery of language, facilitating the essential task of communication allows leaders to articulate their ideas persuasively. It also suggests that those who master technical skills are more likely to be perceived as leaders. Mastery of skill is affirmed by 2 Timothy 2:15, which says, "Study to shew yourself approved unto God a workman that needth not be ashamed, rightly dividing the word of truth." Whether it is the study of God's word or leading in a particular field, as a leader, you must devote time to learning. Lashway's report also states that interpersonal skills are critical to leaders.

As we study the different leadership types, I may, at times, interchangeably use transformational leadership with servant leadership. Both types are interested in creating others like themselves and offer the conceptual framework for dynamic leadership. One of the main distinctions

1

to note between transformational leadership and servant leadership is the focus of the leader. The primary focus of a transformational leader is to motivate others for the organization's greater good. While the servant leader's primary focus is to work to help its followers. We are living in a time when transformational leadership is being praised for increasing organizational satisfaction, commitment, and effectiveness, making it a model worth further study. This is something that we can easily observe ourselves. Consider the leaders you know, are they transformational leaders? Do they demonstrate strong communication skills? Communication skills are important and will be discussed in detail in chapter three.

What is leadership? Many years ago, while enrolled in the school administration program at Fayetteville State University, I was seated amid a diverse population of educators, many of whom had a vast amount of leadership experience in their schools and local communities, when the professor asked this very question, "What is leadership?" Upon hearing this question, hands immediately went up without hesitation. The question sounded straight forward and simple enough. It was one that we all thought we could easily answer. However, it quickly became apparent that this question was more complicated than we had initially thought, as students failed again and again to get the affirmation they hoped to receive. Yes, in this room of aspiring administrators, we once thought we had the answer. However, now, we became more pensive as it neared our turn to answer the question. Some answers were long and drawn out while others were short and more concise. Nonetheless, long or short, every answer was a variation of the same e.g., leadership is being responsible for leading a group or organization; it is the person in charge, one who has a supervisory role; it is the person that commands or directs others and makes things happen, it is the boss or decision-maker for the organization, or it's the person responsible for managing others.

The professor, I will call him Dr. J. F, patiently continued asking one student after the other the same question as he rounded the room. Each time, he would acknowledge them but not finding the answer he thought best, he would say something like, no, that is not exactly what I'm looking for. Remember, every one of us initially thought we had the correct, if not the "best" answer. Nevertheless, he was relentless and continued canvassing the room, seeking yet another definition of leadership. As he continued his quest for his "best" answer, hopes for approval and praise grew dim. The class was at a loss. Why? Because we had heard what was in our mind good descriptions of leadership, so what was left? Then finally, he revealed the one keyword missing from our definitions, he said, "leadership is INFLUENCE!" Wow…what? None of us had thought to define leadership in that manner. Those three simple but powerful words resonated with me. I know you have heard of "ah-ha moments." That was, indeed, my personal "ah-ha" moment. My eyes were wide open, and he had my full attention. I was eager to know more. He continued to explain that influence further is the ability to change the ideas, actions, and opinions of others; in other words, your capacity to get individuals to see things your way. It's the ability to move them from where they are to where they need to be. It all made perfect sense. The truth is that leaders should possess the skill, but it also requires more than an ability or a title to become an effective leader. If you cannot influence others, you will be an ineffective leader and will undoubtedly become frustrated in your efforts. Indeed, leadership has been, is, and will continue to be the ability to influence others.

As a leader, many variables will impact your ability to influence. Some factors will be direct, while others will be indirect. You possess the ability to influence others through your direct relationships with family, friends, and others within your community. Because of your direct contact with them, you can be a primary influencer. In addition to your direct contact, the level of perceived authority or social status also amplifies one's influence. This perceived authority others may have of you can come from your demonstrated experience, education, your communicated knowledge in some area or even from your appearance. On top of that, people are not only influenced by what they know personally about you but also by the opinion's others have about you. Look at these examples: Someone with no direct connection to you may see you and conclude that they dislike you (for reasons of their own) and then share their opinion of you to those within their circle. Their comments about you now have the power too negatively impact your ability to influence within their circle. That is one example of negative indirect influence. Likewise, indirect influence can be positive. For example, someone may think highly of you and openly share their thoughts of praise about you with those in their sphere of influence.

This act of sharing words of admiration about you now impacts your ability to influence them positively.

Note: Indirect influence is not always negative.

People in leadership know the importance of influence and learn techniques for improving their ability to do so. Storytelling is a proven strategy that connects others emotionally to your ideas. Stories evoke feelings of emotions (joy, anger, sadness, urgency…the list goes on) from the hearer. If you don't already utilize storytelling, consider learning how to connect with others using your personal stories or other appropriate stories. You will find that this technique increases your ability to be relatable. Memory experts even teach people to remember names by telling a story around the name. In his book "How Customers Think," Gerald Zaltman, writes that "The mind remembers what it attaches emotion to, and by incorporating stories around facts or perceptions, the memory improves."

Daniel Goleman, the author of "**Social Intelligence**," says every businessperson knows of at least one story of a highly intelligent, highly-skilled person who was promoted to a position of leadership only to encounter failure. Alternatively, they would also be able to recount a story of a person with average intellect and ability who was promoted, and yet, this person soared. Both of these individuals had potential because they both were promoted, and both held the title of leader. However, one failed, and the other succeeded. Considering a few of the things we have covered, what factors may have attributed to the failure of one? Do you think failure could have prevented? If so, how?

TrainingIndustry.com has released its 2019 "Top 20 Leadership Training Companies List." They do this as a part of their commitment to continuously monitor the training marketplace to identify the best providers and services. You can see the full list of ranked providers and services on their site. What would we do without computers and the internet? I don't even want to think about it. Technology is incredible, within a few short seconds and only a few keystrokes, we can have before our eyes a wealth of information. I Googled the "2019 top leadership training companies," and my search quickly found Dale Carnegie still ranked among the top 20. This fact speaks volumes for their continued quality. Companies placed on the Training Industry's list were placed there because they represented unique strengths in their superior training program. Below are a few of the determining criteria used for qualifying companies on the list:

- ➢ influence on the leadership training industry
- ➢ recognition and innovation within the industry
- ➢ vastness of programs and audiences served
- ➢ methods of delivery

Dale Carnegie, a New Yorker, grew up in poverty but became a leading corporate lecturer and author of "How to Win Friends and Influence People." He trained countless people based on the core principle that, "It is possible to change other people's behavior by changing one's behavior toward them." There are many other leadership training programs, however, Dale Carnegie's training process has been around for over a hundred years and continues to be among the elite. Its training and high-quality materials have endured the test of time. At a glance, the core practices, appear to be in alignment or shall I say, have a definite correlation to many behaviors modeled by Christian leaders.

As a lifelong learner, as you continue to study, you will be exposed to a range of ideas. You will encounter many that you will whole-heartedly agree, some in part and then others that you disagree. Some ideas you may refuse to accept based on your values. That is normal; the key is to learn so that you can have choices and make sound decisions. Always be prayerful in your studies, and God will equip you with both discernment and wisdom. I am indeed a witness to that.

Here are just a few of Dale Carnegie's Principles
as listed in "How to Win Friends and Influence People":

CARNEGIE PRINCIPLE	BIBLICAL TRUTH
Don't criticize or condemn	**Luke 6:37** Judge not, and ye shall not be judged: condemn not, and ye shall not be condemned: forgive, and ye shall be forgiven:
Be a good listener	**Proverbs 1:5** "Let the wise hear and increase in learning, and the one who understands obtain guidance."
Talk in terms of the other person's interest	**Philippians 2:4** Look not every man on his own things, but every man also on the things of others.
Give the person a fine reputation to live up to	**Proverbs 10:7** The memory of the righteous is blessed, But the name of the wicked will rot. **Proverbs 22:1** A good name is to be more desired than great wealth, Favor is better than silver and gold.

Cautiously lead others and always remember that there is a line between influencing and manipulating. Satan blurs the lines hoping to seduce leaders into thinking that they are great leaders when, in fact, they have become master manipulators. An influential leader who inspires and motivates others to make conscious decisions is vastly different from manipulators who have mastered the art of conquering people who don't even know when they have been conquered. These manipulators, in essence, are stealing one's God-given right of free will. WARNING! If your leadership takes a turn towards manipulation, you are no longer leading God's way. Repent and start over.

Anyone in leadership will attest to the fact that leadership has its challenges. Every leader will experience some degree of it whenever they step into an organization with an established culture. Or, when trying to establish their own or create a new organizational culture. Years ago, IBM was one of the earlier companies with a recognizable corporate culture. Professionalism, innovation, high customer, and employee satisfaction were at its core. As individuals, we all have our personalities and strange as it sounds; organizations have their personalities as well. It's called organizational culture. How does it happen? It occurs over time and is comprised of values, norms, and tangible objects (are things that can be seen, the physical manifestations such as dress codes, rituals, awards, public displays, logos, furnishings, etc...) and intangible things (behaviors, attitudes and beliefs/values) associated with the organization members and is demonstrated by their actions. It does not take members long to sense the culture of a place. Although you may not be able to describe it precisely, you can feel it. Culture is one of those things you can sense.

When the stressful demand for high profit creates the organization's culture, those factors can outweigh production quality, integrity, and can adversely affect the treatment of its entire team. Nonetheless, Christian leaders in any work environment should make it better. Their presence should positively impact environments. Even in the worst of situations, their behaviors will not be adding toxicity to it. They will speak and be respected for their truth and not viewed as complainers. All leaders are expected to be able to not only identifying problems but also finding viable solutions as well as knowing the importance of leaving personal issues out of the workplace.

Note: always be aware of the work environment and its impact on you. If your CORE values are in constant conflict with your work, it can manifest in your job performance and your health. What options do you have? What is in your best interest?

Joel Olsten wrote of a woman who had lost her home in Hurricane Katrina (2005). This woman had a legitimate issue to complain. However, she chose to thank God that she was alive and that her family was doing well. Although she endured sweltering heat without the comforts of A/C and electricity, she had hope, joy, and peace, and confidence that God was working things out for her. This woman made the conscious decision to take this devastating moment in her life and *reframe* it. She chose to turn it around, refusing to feel self-pity or to allow the adverse circumstances to consume her. When you are able to do this, regardless of your situation, it demonstrates that you have disciplined your mind to reflect on Romans 8:28 (KJV), "And we know that all things work together for good to them that love God, to them who are the called according to his purpose." This ability will enable you to soar high above the storm while others are being tossed and driven. First Thessalonians 5:18 says, "give thanks in all circumstances, for this is God's will in Christ Jesus for you." Remember, it is God's will for us to be thankful in every situation; we should endeavor to see everything from His perspective. What are some possible ways you can bring positivity to a negative work environment? How can you help others reframe their negative statements? Perhaps, you can point out something positive that may have been overlooked to diffuse the situation. Or, refrain from adding more incendiary comments. Any of those strategies may prove helpful.

If looking for a role model, Jesus is our perfect example of a servant leader. He was always concerned about the welfare of others without regard to their social status. While living His life here on earth, Jesus never lost sight of His mission. Even in the most difficult times, He was always responsive to the present circumstance of those He was enlisting to join Him. He never once failed in His concern for others or once lost focus of His primary objective, which was to redeem lost souls from sin. Some folk mistakenly equate good leadership with power and the ability to make others conform to their demands. In my mind, this is reminiscent of a bully's mentality. History has shown us many instances of leaders who lead by force and fear. This bully approach can get the job done for a while but often has others feeling angry, oppressed, and subjugated.

> Note: a compliant team is not the most effective or most productive team.

These teams can become rebellious or passive-aggressive. Jesus described himself as gentle and humble. "Take My yoke upon you and learn from Me, for I am gentle and humble in heart, and you will find rest for your souls." (Matthew 11:29 NASB) Matthew 11:29, KJV uses the word meek, and the NIV says gentle. Some people erroneously associate these words with weakness. Jesus was clearly saying anything but weak. He was demonstrating that His Godly manhood had all power and all authority, but it was subject to HIS control. Meekness is not a weakness, but it is power under control. When Christian leaders have the indwelling of the Holy Spirit, they desire to be more like Jesus, meek, and humble. These leaders are not typically combative or hostile, which is the propensity of a sinful nature. They continuously employ the Holy Spirit to keep their power subjected to its control. Their willingness to yield to the Holy Spirit allows them to remain focused on the fulfillment of God's perfect will and not unwisely act out of their emotions.

During Jesus' time on earth, there was never an instance when He used His power or authority for personal gain. Jesus never sought to create an agenda that differed from His primary assignment, nor did He flaunt His divine position. His primary objective was irrefutably to carry out the will of God. I know with all my talk of meekness and control, some of you already are thinking about when Jesus entered into the temple, became angry and overturned the tables (Mark 11:15). This behavior was an exception and was not His normal behavior. You too will have times when you must stand boldly for what you believe is right. Allow the Holy Spirit to guide your actions, and you will do the right thing at the right time.

According to Final 1: Attributed Qualities of Leadership Roles by Shelah Rote and Megan Gallagher, our behavior is often modified depending on the situation. Therefore, both leadership and submission roles have their benefit. Leaders must determine which role gives them a better advantage. Rote and Gallagher also pointed out that leadership takes work. Not only must leaders work to gain their position, but they must also continue working to maintain the earned leadership position. As with most things, there are some exceptions. Occasionally, there will be instances when situations will thrust leadership upon you; however, in this book, we will not focus on that type of leadership acquisition.

"Is leadership biological?" My answer is that some people naturally seem to possess both the inclination and ability to lead, but leadership skills can also be learned. How do you become a better leader? Dale Carnegie offers this thought. He says to increase your influence; you should be slow to criticize and complain. As believers, we know that we are to possess the fruit of the Spirit as shown in Galatians 5:22-23; "22But the fruit of the Spirit is love, joy, peace, longsuffering, gentleness, goodness, faith, 23Meekness, temperance: against such there is no law." We also know that a complaining spirit is not a desired characteristic. Generally speaking, continually complaining, unsatisfied people can be contentious and quarrelsome. These people become bitter over time, are challenging to work with, and will undermine the efforts of their organizations.

There is a tremendous amount of responsibility resting upon a leader's shoulder. Their temperament, tone, pace, and expectations will set the pace for the organization, and followers will reflect their leadership. Sadly, a whiny- complaining leader will, unfortunately, have followers that demonstrate those same undesirable behaviors. The point to remember is that leaders will experience many stressful situations, but their ongoing challenge will be to keep things in the proper perspective and stay positive. The Bible encourages us to think about good things. Thinking good thoughts, in essence, will reduce, if not totally, eliminate complaining. Philippians 4:8 (KJV) says, "Finally, brethren, whatsoever things are true, whatsoever things are honest, whatsoever things are, whatsoever things are pure, whatsoever things are lovely, whatsoever things are of good report; if there be any virtue, and if there be any praise, think on these things." Nonetheless, there may be times under duress from internal or external pressures, that leaders may fall victim to complaining. When that happens to you, be resilient. Make a concerted effort to bounce back as quickly as possible, forgive yourself and move forward. Beware of the times when you contemplate wrongfully assigning blame to others because you are resisting holding yourself accountable.

As a leader, your name will be attached to the organization's outcomes, good or bad. It is your responsibility, to be honest, objective, and focused. When things happen, focus, and think. Ask yourself, "What went well or what went wrong?" Leading with a positive attitude does not mean that you are oblivious to negative happenings that may be occurring. Nor does it mean that you are looking at the world through th e proverbial rose-colored glasses. Not at all. It means that you have a sharp sense of awareness, you are cognizant of what is Even if you temporarily lose financially because of your ethical decision, you will ultimately gain inner peace within. Though the prospects of recognition from others did not drive your moral action, others will learn of it and respect you for your integrity. You will have contributed to making the world a better place.

The Bible records Adam complaining to God in the garden after he disobeyed. To justify his wrong, he said, "The woman whom thou gavest to be with me, she gave me of the tree, and I did eat." (Genesis 3:12) Another example is King David, a man after God's own heart. David complained when he said, "Why do the heathen rage, and the people imagine a vain thing?" (Psalm 2:1). This scripture passage lets us know that even when you are close to God, you must still be vigilant. Remember that constant grumbling and complaining is counterproductive. But, if you happen to miss the mark, keep the primary objective in focus, and remind yourself of Philippians 4:8. Your thoughts matter, so get your mind right. When unpleasant situations arise, and they will, you will be ready to lead those necessary critical discussions. Never undervalue the importance of open, honest communication. Times of conflict allow you to practice exercising wisdom and utilizing prompts to promote constructive dialogue. It is necessary to address unpleasant matters at the onset before matters worsen.

The way you address important topics impacts your reputation, credibility, and your response received from listeners. Instead of an indiscriminate verbal lashing (and yes, sometimes you may feel it is well-warranted), pause. Pausing will give room for the emotional attachment to the issue to subside. You never want your emotions to derail your delivery. Pausing also gives you additional time to coherently organize your thoughts before jumping into action. People are listening so be cognizant of all your conversations. Make sure you always incorporate the elements of a good speech. Start with a clear beginning, content-rich middle, and a strong conclusion. I am going to ask this question, but it is rhetorical. Have you ever had to listen to someone who is all over the place? They start their conversation, running out of the gate with no context clues, and it is apparent that they have no clear beginning. The middle gets even muddier, and it seems as if they miss every possible opportunity to wrap it up and end it. Conversations like these leave you exhausted and still unsure of the main point. Don't let this be you.

Let's do a quick review on how to give unpleasant feedback. Always pause and think before speaking. Carefully, organize your thoughts as you will want every advantage in communicating your concerns in the best possible light for the desired results.

Things to Remember:

Timing is Key. Once you have identified the importance of a matter, your next consideration should be the question of "timing." When is the best time to address it? Should you act now or wait for additional information? If there is no better time than now, how do you forge ahead and get to the root as quickly as possible to prevent further damage?

Blurting out your dissatisfaction in an open forum when it only applies to one or two can be counterproductive. Instead, you might consider scheduling a one-on-one meeting with those involved. However, if the intent is to stop a high probability of similar behaviors by others, leaders will opt to do differently. In this case, they may choose an open setting. Either way, ask yourself, "What would Jesus do?" Would He be pleased with your actions? Answering these questions will create an atmosphere for a much more productive meeting for all involved.

Be Specific. Specificity is critical when your goal is to improve anything. Here, I am reminded of Habakkuk 2:2 "...write the vision and make it plain..." This verse is very applicable to your leadership. There will be times when you must lay it all out, be specific in the details, call out names when needed, and be exact when telling of particular incidences. Don't mince words or be ambiguous. While sitting here, I had a flashback of my pre-retirement days and my many years' classroom observations. It didn't happen often, but I have witnessed teachers' directives being ignored unless they specifically called out the particular student's name. Now, tell me how that works. Were the students so preoccupied with what they were doing that they were oblivious to the teacher's directives, or were they demonstrating passive-aggressiveness? Were they saying, "They didn't call my name, so it doesn't apply to me?" Hmmm, do you think this type of scenario is limited to the four-walled classroom? Unfortunately, it is not. During your lifetime of serving in a leadership capacity, there will be situations when adults will act just like those students in the classroom. Therefore, you must be able to identify whom to call out for your directives to be followed. Being direct and specific helps make them accountable. It eliminates the, "Oh, did you mean me?" excuse. Moreover, in your leading, you must never forget who you need to lead you. Stay before Him and ask for wisdom, understanding, and the strength to get the job done. It is an enormous task before you when you lead others. It can be very draining, but it is also very rewarding. People are depending on you and rely on your sound judgment, insight, and foresight.

Each day is different and will hold its challenges, the best you can do is your best. There will be days while working in your leadership capacity; that you will feel like you are just barely holding on. If that's what you are feeling it's real, keep holding on. I know all too well that working with people can be mentally and emotionally draining. Contending with changing personalities in an organization can take its toll on you. Maybe you have never experienced it, one minute all is well, then, the very next moment there is a total shift. Regardless of the disposition of others, you must learn to manage your emotions and maintain your objectivity. If you become angry and your annoyance and irritation ends up manifesting with such intensity that the point you are trying to make is lost, your cause has already been defeated. The Bible reminds us to focus on the facts. Philippians 4:8 KJV says, The Bible tells us to focus on the facts. Philippians 4:8 KJV says, "Finally, brethren, whatsoever things are true, whatsoever things are honest, whatsoever things are just, whatsoever things are pure, whatsoever things are lovely, whatsoever things are of good report; if there be any virtue, and if there be any praise, think on these things."

This scripture passage will have a calming effect and assist you in conveying your message with sound reasoning. Pausing will give you time to gather yourself emotionally and organize your thoughts. Then, plainly state the importance of resolving the problem. Be ready to recommend preventative actions to ensure the issue of concern does not continue as a repetitive occurrence.

Focus on the Positives (remember, "if there be any virtue..."). In some instances, it may be a daunting, seemingly impossible mission. However, the good news is, it's not; you can do it. If you look hard enough, you can find something. Do your best to remain positive. A positive outlook softens the blow of the criticism and shows that you are aware of the good as well. You may consider utilizing the sandwich approach when delivering a stern critique. The "sandwich approach" method of feedback for an evaluation is first to share something positive, then, state the negative which needs corrective action followed by another positive. This ends the feedback on a positive note and leaves the person willing, if not eager, to accept your suggested changes. This level of cooperation fosters goodwill and does not require the leader to demand change. Good leaders will want decisions to be accepted because of their understood validity, not merely because of the leader's authority. A good leader will look for ways to move reluctant compliance towards enthused consensus.

> Note: Compliance alone does not foster optimum performance. If there is no agreement on understood validity, compliance will suffice temporarily to sustain some forward movement for the organization.

Some leaders are entirely convinced and that the "Sandwich" approach yields the best results. However, others disagree, and I will give you an example of that, as well. Remember, this book is designed to equip you with strategies that I believe will aid you in "Leading God's Way." You are to select the strategies that resonate with you and compliment your style. I will provide the ideas and resources for your toolbox; you decide what works best for you. One noted opposing view of the sandwich approach is by Roger Schwarz. He is the organizational psychologist and leadership team consultant that wrote an article in the Harvard Business Review (2013), "The Sandwich Approach Undermines Your Feedback." Schwarz says the "Sandwich Approach" is unilaterally controlling because the person giving the feedback is trying to create the desired outcome.

He supports being fully transparent and calls for a "Mutual Learning Approach," which he believes to be more productive.

First, the "Mutual Learning Approach" increases the probability that it will be a discovery experience. Second, everyone will know the planned sequence of the meeting and can jointly work to keep the meeting on track. Finally, by expressing that you may lack some information and may in some degree have contributed to the problem, you shift the meeting from one of critiquing others to one in which all of you are exploring together what happened. Also, now, you are planning together how to move forward. Schwarz believes negative feedback transparency means respecting others and not controlling or alienating them. Furthermore, he thought that it made negative or positive feedback more genuine, resulting in a lower level of discomfort and anxiety.

When you have concerns that must be addressed, do your due diligence to get a thorough assessment of the situation. Be proactive and gather as much information as you can to ensure sound decision-making. We know that decisions are only as good as the information used to make them. I recall the regular practice scenarios would be given during leadership training. Each student would get their assignment sheet called "inbox basket" scenarios. These "inbox box" scenarios were simulated real-life situations that were to jog our critical thinking and develop our decision-making processes. The scenarios would address many different issues, school policy, law, ethics, etc. We were charged with coming up with solutions or ways to mitigate the problems based on the information at hand. We were advised, when you have to make a "NOW' decision, use caution and say, based on the information I have at this time..." Saying this gives you the latitude to change your answer when more information has been made available and ensures your credibility is maintained. And of course, all solutions had to be legal.

YOUR LEADERSHIP WILL REFLECT YOUR CONFIDENCE IN YOUR COMPETENCE

Essential questions to ask to ensure sound decision-making:

What are the facts?

Can you find a positive?

What will work and how can you move forward?

What are the challenges?

Do you have the needed resources and personnel?

How can you reduce or eliminate the barriers?

Remember this; it is crucial to stay positive when holding any position of leadership. When leaders are confident and can retain their optimism, they are naturally more resilient. This resiliency will enable them to bounce back from setbacks swiftly. Don't you love the sound of that? I certainly do! We all know that trials will inevitably come, but your ability to recover quickly is undoubtedly a crucial attribute of any successful leader. The quicker you can get yourself together, the faster you can re-enter the race. Never, never quit, and keep moving forward.

Leaders should strive to be authentic and generous with their show of appreciation towards others. Also, it is equally important that they are readily available to evaluate situations and offer their honest, constructive feedback. As we know, if the feedback is truly honest, it will not always be positive; but, it is necessary if there is an expectation of continuous improvement. Conversely, if a leader has established good rapport within the organization or team and has shown a sufficient amount of appreciation over time, their negative feedback will not be seen as a lack of recognition of past work. Research indicates that low performance is a problematic indicator of under-appreciated people. Therefore, when people feel undervalued for their effort, they tend to be less motivated, thus, developing an increasing lack of interest in accomplishing tasks with excellence or at their maximum capability. With this in mind, it's advantageous for leaders to learn how to show genuine appreciation whenever opportunities present themselves. The ability to show others gratitude and knowing when and how to correct them in a manner that maintains their dignity will prove to be an asset to you. Development in this area is invaluable and will garner you added respect and loyalty from your team. Commit today to begin cultivating your gratitude quotient?

As we continue our leadership journey, you will see that being a leader is an ongoing learning process. There is no one size fits all model. In Michelle Obama's book, "Becoming," she makes mention that some people look at becoming "as if at some point, you become something, and that's the end of it." I agree with her that becoming is an ongoing process. Any person, particularly one in leadership, who stops learning, will soon become an ineffective leader. I challenge you to commit to continuous learning. Be the leader that is always growing, always mentoring, always developing, always moving towards the divine destiny God has designed for you. Yes, be an evolving leader, one who is always "BECOMING!" Be the kind of leader who prepares successors to take your place as you move from one level to the next. I challenge you to see yourself as perpetually "Becoming." Becoming what? becoming a better leader, becoming a more knowledgeable leader, becoming a more respected leader, becoming the one who is demonstrating "Leading God's Way!" The world is waiting for you; the world needs you. Make your commitment today.

Group dynamics, is a term coined by Kurt Lewin, a social psychologist, can be fragile. Lewin observed that when people worked in groups, they adopted certain behaviors or roles associated with the nature of the work and or the personalities within the group. These unconscious psychological factors affect each person in the group individually and the group as a whole unit. When a new person enters a group, they can alter the entire environment. Good leaders are keenly perceptive and will notice these changes. Then they may find it necessary to restate and clarify job duties, increase the frequency of communication, or even implement new strategies to maintain the desired work environment climate and general productivity.

Some people instinctively become very defensive when critiqued. Understandably, there are varying degrees of this, and it is more noticeable in some than others. This natural predisposition to be defensive makes some averse to accepting fault. Therefore, leaders who fail to recognize this fail to understand the impact of their message delivery. And when they speak in an insensitive manner, they unwittingly create an unwanted hostility. Thus, fostering an environment of disconnected, disgruntled, employees. Leaders who possess low emotional intelligence will ultimately cause their organization to suffer. However, once the problem has been identified, the process for restoration should begin. Although this can be costly and time-consuming, it is a worthwhile investment to strengthen internal organizational relationships. Let's call it a necessity for any forward-moving organization to repair the damage created by poor leadership. I cannot overemphasize how important it is to know your staff. So, take the time to learn what matters to them and to understand what motivates them. This information will help you better understand how they will respond. This essential knowledge is needed to ensure that your message is clear, not easily misconstrued, and is one they can relate.

Do you realize that words are containers of our thoughts? They give meaning to our ideas and are the foundation of all that happens. Jesus was teaching a great multitude by the sea side in Mark 4:1-2 using stories to convey his doctrine, His words entered into their spirits. Yes, His words were the vehicle that carried His thoughts to their spirit. Jesus always used His words for good and we, too, possess these word containers. We can build up or tear down those we encounter while on this life's journey. The Bible tells us that "death and life are in the power of the tongue, and those who love it will eat its fruit," Proverbs 18:21. Whether we believe it or not, within each of us, God has given us formidable power. Yes, you and I have the power to bless or blame, cure, or curse. You and I possess the ability to heal with our words or kill the spirits of others. This God-given power rests in our tongues. Take a moment to think about how you speak; what words are you using? How are you using your power? What are your word containers carrying? Are they full of life or death? Are you building up those around you or are you tearing them down? Do you find yourself blessing or blaming? Are you curing or cursing? I find it unfortunate that some leaders delight in their ability to cause others to feel doubt and insecurity. These immature leaders love it when others question the value of their contributions. Why? Because this somehow makes immature leaders feel superior. Make it a point never to be that kind of leader.

God has given each of us freedom of choice and allows us to make our own decisions in all things. What is the purpose of this freedom, and how does it play into our leadership role? God wants us to willingly choose to lead others in a manner that is in alignment with His teachings — understanding that we can invoke the blessings of God in our lives and the lives of others. Or, we can choose to speak curses against ourselves and them. He desires that we always speak the truth in love and to declare our truth boldly even in difficult times. It is our responsibility to learn to be cognizant about what we say and how we use our words for they will undoubtedly impact our future. Admittedly, this will not always be easy to do. Exercise restraint and use discipline as you allow WORDS to flow from your lips.

Amy Morin, a psychotherapist, and lecturer at Northeastern University note that a leader who is comfortable showing gratitude creates a healthy culture in the workplace and boosts morale. That's right; a simple show of appreciation is one of the cheapest things a leader can do to lift spirits and boost morale. This morale booster doesn't have to cost one single dime. However, many leaders are reluctant to do so. Why? Because some leaders mistakenly feel that praise for a job well-done may inflate the employee's self-esteem causing a decline in future performance. Or, that it may ultimately cost them money should the employee think they deserve a raise for their job performance. In the book Servant Leadership in Action: How You Can Achieve Great Relationships and Results, Tom Mullins writes, "Celebrating your people demonstrates that you value them, and you acknowledge their part in making the victory possible. This affirms them and promotes continued productivity. Others who lead may believe that a good job is what they hired the employee to do; therefore, there is no need to express additional thanks to employees for merely doing what they were hired to do. Where do you stand? Are you the leader who only mentions poor job performance to those you are supervising and rarely offer praise for a job well done? Or, are you the leader who has developed a strong relationship with your team and routinely provide them with both positive or negative feedback? Always remember, the people on your team need to know where they stand. How do they learn that? They learn it from your feedback.

A leader's honest feedback ensures that the assignment is clear and helps the team's future performance. Will every leader benefit from developing the art of providing honest feedback? Absolutely. An underperforming team member may become resentful, more oppositional, and do even less when leaders marginalize them. You do not have to marginalize people when correcting them. Use caution; don't think people will miss it if you feel they are insignificant. It will come across in your speech, tone, and maybe even in your body gestures. As a leader seeking to lead God's way, you can be firm and corrective but still be respectful. No one wants to feel marginalized. Of course, some leaders believe that belittling comments provokes followers to excellence. And, it may be true that some people temporarily are spurred to work harder when they are angry, or they may set out to prove that they can earn the respect of that leader. However, this book is all about doing it God's way. Therefore, our goal is to correct others in a manner that gets the job done while still being considerate of them. May I suggest you keep in mind and apply the Golden Rule. This well-known verse passage in Matthew 7:12 (KJV) is a useful measuring tool for us, "Therefore all things whatsoever ye would that men should do to you: do ye even so to them: for this is the law and the prophets."

Great leaders are an inspiration to others and know that there are times when they must consider other perspectives to understand a situation fully. Never forget that a leader's success greatly depends on their ability to influence others. How good are you in determining the needs and desires of your subordinates? Are you taking the time to discover what motivates them? What can you do to get a better idea of their needs and wants? When you know these things, you can successfully motivate others, and you will be on your way to becoming a better leader. One essential key to increasing your influence, according to Dale Carnegie, is to show a genuine interest in others. This is of particular importance today when so many people habitually show little regard for others. People desire to be seen, heard, and valued.

When you are a leader who leads God's way, people appreciate your transparency and authentic show of interest. Many have become distrustful of leaders who seem over eager to ingratiate themselves to garner friendships. A genuine pleasant smile from someone who actively listens goes a long way. Another thing that Dale Carnegie noted is that people appreciate a leader who takes the time to remember names. When you take the time to remember someone's name or try to learn how to pronounce it correctly, you are indirectly saying, I value you, you matter to me. Your name is worth remembering. Admittedly, I have never been great in this area of name recall, but I try because I do know how it makes me feel when someone has taken the time and remembers to use my preferred name. For example, when asked my name, I always say, "Jacqueline." It makes me smile when I meet them again, and they say "Hello, Jacqueline" and they have not shortened it to say, "Hello, Jackie." Why? Because they took the time to remember that "Jacqueline" is the name I had given them. I gave it to them that way because it is my preferred name, but especially in the workplace or a professional setting and definitely when it's being printed. Of course, with family, friends or in informal settings, an abbreviated version is often used.

Dale Carnegie cautions us to be courteous when talking with others, reminding us not to monopolize conversations. Have you ever have been in a conversation and found it challenging to get a word because the other person was talking so much? They pause briefly only to get a gulp of air so that they can continue. Or, are you having to jump in, to add your comment or response? Then, when you finally get to say something, they keep talking on as if you have said nothing. How does this make you feel? Can you see the importance of being courteous when talking to others? Can you see how it can shape one's opinion?

NOTE: CONVERSATIONS ARE NOT PRESENTATIONS. INCLUDE THE LISTENER!

As a leader with a wealth of knowledge and often captive audiences, it may take some effort for you to dial it back a little. Nonetheless, you will be well-served to begin practicing developing better listening skills. Encourage others to talk more by asking them open-ended questions that require more than a yes or no answer. Coach them to say more by showing genuine interest and asking more questions. In this way, they become comfortable sharing their thoughts with you.

We already know that leaders want to speak and to be heard, but great leaders will take the time to listen. Not only should you actively listen to what is being said, but, you should also listen for what they may not be saying. What does this mean? It means that when a person is talking, be attune to the clues they are sending with their body language and tone. Learning these nonverbal cues will assist you in getting a clearer picture of the person's true feelings. It is a known fact that much of our nonverbal signaling is an automatic response and done unconsciously. These nonverbal cues we send can have us unwittingly communicating a great deal of information. Observant people can learn much about our state of mind and our true feelings by noticing our facial expressions or watching our hand gestures and other body language. The position in which we hold our bodies also be a clue. Amazing– I guess this supports the saying, "A picture is worth a thousand words." This is a good time to ask your friends and family to tell what it is that you do when you are angry? Irritated? Impatient? Happy? Trust me, they can tell you. And when they do, don't be in denial just believe them. They know!!! Then remember those tell-tell giveaways in future situations when you don't want nonverbal cues to give you away.

If the researchers have it right, and if 60% to 90% of our communication is nonverbal, it is to our benefit to know more about these signs. We need to make sure we don't look disingenuous by having words that are not in agreement with our body language.

LEADING GOD'S WAY

Below samples of body language and how they are interpreted:

Positive Indicators	
Body Language Signs	**Meaning**
Relaxed posture	indicates that you are comfortable with the people that you are with or in the setting you are in.
Leaning forward	shows interest and that you are listening
Crossed arms	can indicate that you are not open to what is being said or you are turned off by the surroundings
Hand gestures	can be used for emphasis and authority when they are purposeful. Otherwise, they can be flailing distractions.
Firm handshakes	signals confidence, whereas, a flimsy or light handshake can send a message of timidity or weakness.
Eye contact	denotes interest in the person or topic (However; in some cultures, direct eye contact is a sign of disrespect. Cultural sensitivity is needed.)
Affirmative movements	show agreement (nodding of the head or smiling)
Negative Indicators	
Watching the clock	you don't want to be there, you have something more important to do, or you are short on time.
Anxiously looking away	translates as shy or disinterested.
Repeated touching of the face	lying
Restless hands	hands are continually pulling or picking at something shows boredom.
Tapping, whether it's your finger, toes, or a pen	indicates a degree of stress or impatience. It is also annoying to the listener.
No Fake Smiles	an authentic smile comes from more than your mouth. Your entire face, particularly the eyes, reflect a genuine smile. If you must put on a smile think of a happy memory so that the rest of your face will agree. ;-)

Note: Personal Space is needed whenever we are speaking to people, but particularly when speaking to those outside of your intimate circle. When speaking to unfamiliar people, use 3-4 feet as your standard. If people start backing up while you are talking to them, you are too close. Pay attention to the signs.

Being a person of influence is one of the many traits of a mature leader. A "mature leader" is usually a person with a high degree of emotional intelligence. The Harvard Business Review has hailed emotional intelligence as "a ground-breaking, paradigm-shattering idea." Companies now routinely evaluate emotional intelligence when hiring, promoting, and developing their employees. They believe that this trait increases the probability of a leader's success. The ability to connect with others and show your humanity lends itself to improving your influence. There is no perfect leader, so when you make mistakes own them, apologize when necessary, and move forward. Don't deny or lie to cover up mistakes and don't try to assert the blame onto someone else. People will know when you try to avoid liability, and you will ultimately lose credibility. Shifting blame to others for your failures is a sign of immaturity as a leader. Every mature leader understands that at the end of the day, their team's failure or success lies in their hands. It is a huge responsibility, but leaders must be willing to accept this responsibility when a failure occurs. Good leaders are gatherers of facts. These are some questions a responsible leader might ask when thoughtfully reviewing a situation:

1. Could the failure have been anticipated?

2. If so, what were the signs?

3. What could have prevented it?

4. Were the right people assigned to the job?

5. Did those responsible for doing the job have the proper training?

6. Were they equipped with all of the materials and supplies needed to be successful?

7. Was the progress monitored closely enough?

8. Should they have received additional support to ensure the desired outcome?

9. What did we learn from this situation?

10. How will this information ensure that future attempts are successful?

11. What will we do differently?

Although first impressions can be incorrect, they have a powerful lasting effect. Would you like to be summed up in a glance? It is done more often that we realize. It is incredible to me, and I must say, it doesn't seem quite fair that some people, at a glance, are viewed as having the "right stuff" for leadership while others are quickly discounted.

There is a great example of this in the Bible, when Samuel was searching for a king, the Bible says (Samuel 16:6), "When they arrived, Samuel saw Eliab and thought, 'Surely the Lord's anointed stands here before the Lord.'" Samuel had immediately been taken in by Eliab's physique. Eliab, no doubt, looked like someone who could command authority and respect. [7]"But the Lord said to Samuel, 'Do not consider his appearance or his height, for I have rejected him.'" Can you recall a time when you have formed an opinion of someone because of their appearance, their verbal ability, or the lack thereof? Have you ever been judged wrongly because of how people perceived you because of the way you look? People look at the outward appearance, but the Lord looks at the heart. Isn't it great that He judges the heart?

There are all types of leaders. You see them every day. Some charismatic leaders are striking in build; beautiful or very handsome; while others may be attractive because they exude an innate air of confidence and naturally possesses a winning personality. We do know that society looks at outward appearances, thinking that these factors elevate levels of influence. And in some instances, it can affect influence. It is a natural expectation that leaders with the above attributes would appear to have the upper hand by their innate disposition and external looks. We also know that leaders without the advantage of the traits mentioned above can still be outstanding leaders who are very effective in their leadership role. Regardless, of your level of experience or current ability, always be open to learn and improve. Continuous learning will enhance your capacity to influence, and influence is the power that fuels leadership.

Most leaders choose to think they are great leaders because they have the title, and things are getting done. On the contrary, some admittedly weak leaders can have the title yet have a team that consistently manages to get things done. How is that possible? Many variables make it possible. Some weak leaders are fortunate enough to have someone on their team who possesses the power of influence and ensure that the job gets done. This person is the one who is turning the wheels for the leader. For the sake of this book, I will refer to these employees as the "wheel turners." These are the behind the scenes folk, you may not know their names, but you know their work. They may be under-appreciated or unrecognized for their contributions, but the quality of their work does not change. When recognized for their value, it may not be their leader. Usually, they are not encouraged to seek roles that would garner more pay and authority by their leader. Why? Because they are the one that is making things happen for the leader and make the leader's job easy.

> Note: A mature leaders want to promote people of high caliber and reward their loyalty.

In many cases, the immature leader will feel uncomfortable sharing credit or his/her authority and knowledge with others. This leader may be slightly insecure and feel threatened that recognition given to the "wheel turner" would undermine their control. In some cases, the "wheel turner" may not even desire a title such as a supervisor or a manager. These "wheel turner's" are content working behind the scenes and making things happen for others. Recognize them and show your appreciation for their dedication and work ethic.

Below you have been provided a list of **CORE VALUES.** Stop now and select (3) that resonate with you or that you feel are a good fit for your organization. You may be tempted to select more but narrow it down to three. It will help you narrow your focus on your mission. Also, remember there is no right or wrong selection.

Dependability
Reliability
Loyalty
Commitment
Open-mindedness
Consistency
Honesty
Efficiency
Innovation
Creativity
Good humor
Compassion
Spirit of adventure
Motivation
Positivity
Optimism
Passion
Respect
Fitness
Courage
Education
Perseverance
Patriotism
Service to others
Environmentalism

Did you find it difficult to narrow your selection down to two or three? If you still have more than three, see if some of the CORE VALUES you have selected are similar. If they are, start an elimination process until the one that resonates with you most is left. Repeat this process until you have narrowed it down to two or three. List them here

1_____

2_____

3_____

Explain why you selected these three as your CORE Values.

_____

_____

_____

_____

_____

_____

_____

_____

_____

_____

_____

_____

_____

_____

_____

_____

CHAPTER 2

*7*ypes of *L*eaders

"Don't waste your time arguing with people that have no power or authority over you."
Judge Mablean Ephraim

According to Eagly and Johnson, there is a distinct difference in leadership style when comparing the leadership styles of men and women. Their studies revealed that female leaders generally led others more democratically and interpersonally. However, both types of leaders can skillfully facilitate the development of strategies that effectively improve the communication of a shared vision. This reflects excellence and equity. When people are in a leadership role (male or female), the reasonable expectation is that they will demonstrate integrity and behave ethically, thereby, building community through collaboration, team building, problem-solving, and shared decision-making. Female leaders frequently incorporate collaboration and caregiving, which reflects a "**bottom-up**" rather than a "**top-down**" leadership style. Effective leaders must be confident and **adroit** enough to acknowledge that there will be times when an assertive and forceful leadership is the only prudent strategy. Accordingly, although you may have a preferred leadership style, you must recognize when a circumstance dictates a switch or shift. Although this change may only last for a short while, you must be willing and able to adjust your style in order to be the most effective.

In this chapter, we will discuss nine different leadership styles. Some leadership styles tend to be more prevalent in one or the other gender, Eagly and Johnson (1990). With others, have no particular correlation or preference based on gender. However, some leadership styles are more suitable than others depending on the industry or organization. For example, the rigid authoritarian leadership needed in the military probably is not the style best suited in areas of research or a highly creative environment. The Laissez-faire or Participative leadership style that may help a magazine editor thrive and rise to the top may not work well for the leader trying to excel in the manufacturing industry. Different styles for different places, it all makes sense. This lets you know that there is not a one size (style) fits all leader. With this being said, it is imperative for you to know your style. If your preferred style matches the position which you are working in, the probability of your success will be higher. If it doesn't, you may be prone to both elevated work stress and low achievement.

Transactional Leadership is a style that is focused on supervision and performance. This term refers to transacting, conducting or carrying out. These leaders operate by establishing and adhering to a precise protocol that usually has a clear chain of command. They implement a future reward approach to gain compliance and completion of management activities. Transactional leaders offer an exchange of rewards for good performance. As a form of punishment, they withhold rewards to those who are in the wrong or underperforming. Although this can be an effective way to operate, employees are not intrinsically motivated and seldom reach their full creative ability under this leadership model.

A Transformative Leader has the ability to inspire, train and equip those around them and appear to have a more lasting impact on those they lead. They will encourage their team to grow and eagerly celebrate accomplishments which fosters team confidence. They are ranked high as leaders and are in great demand by organizations. When a Transformative Leader is away for short periods of time, their team retains its ability to operate productively. Therefore, the organization continues to move forward. These highly sought-after leaders use their transformational ability as they cast their organization's vision. Some studies indicate that women are more transformational in their leadership style than their male counterparts. Do you agree that women seem to empower others more, are more democratic, and tend to be more nurturing? Do they use personal contact to enhance interpersonal relationship to influence their followers? What evidence have you seen? How do you think this ability is an asset to the organization?

For many females, connecting to, caring for, and taking responsibility for the needs of others, indicate a certain sense of success (Chodoro 1974: Miller 1976; Gilligan 1982). They use their communication skills and their emotional intelligence to create an environment that is conducive to independent rational thinking. Leading researchers, Peter Salovey, psychologist; and John D. Mayer define emotional intelligence as the ability to recognize and understand one's emotions and the emotions of others. Accordingly, these leaders are thought to be able to easily move organizations forward. Why is that? Because they understand the value of equipping and empowering others to become leaders themselves? Can it be that women more selfless than men? It seems so according to research data which confirms that women have a higher propensity for putting the needs of others above their own (Axelrod 1984). Males, in comparison, are more directive and goal-oriented. Also, according to this study, they are frequently competitive, controlling, and self-reliant. In addition, men were found to prefer power more intensely than women and used their formal position of authority to control people with little hesitation. In a Harvard Business article written by Jack Zenger and Joseph Folkman (June 25, 2019) titled, Research: Women Score Higher Than Men in Most Leadership Skills, found that women still score higher in collaboration and teamwork that their male counterparts. According to this analysis of capabilities that differentiate excellent leaders from average or poor ones, the men outscored women in only two areas 1) technical expertise and 2) develop strategic perspective. This same report indicated that women outscored men on 17 of the 19 competencies. I will mention just a few, 1) champions change, 2) developing others, 3) builds relationships and 4) innovation. You will notice that these are the same competencies necessary for transformational leadership. Nonetheless, there are similarities between women and men regarding leadership and data proves that these similarities outweigh their differences (Tramontin 1993; Lawrence 1998; Nicholson 1996; Doyle and Paludi 1998).

A Transformational Leader pairs well with detail-oriented individuals who not only help implement the transformational leader's strategic vision but are also adept in keeping the goal focus in view. One significant advantage of transformative leaders is that they can help team members envision the future. They lead by example and are wholly committed to what they say and do.

Servant Leadership is one of my personal preferences; perhaps, because of its transformational nature or maybe because Jesus' ministry was a foundation of servanthood. He was our best role model and flawlessly demonstrated how to be a servant leader and continues to do so through His Word. In John 4:13, we see Jesus showing humility as He washed the feet of the disciples. Here, He was demonstrating by example that His disciples should also serve. The willingness of Jesus Christ to put aside his royal majesty was an extreme example of servanthood. Jesus went on to show us one of the strongest examples of servanthood when He washes his disciples' feet in John, Chapter 13:12-17 NIV. Even those in Christ's inner circle had to be taught this important lesson of Servanthood. 12. "When He had finished washing their feet, He put on his clothes and returned to his place. 'Do you understand what I have done for you? He asked them. 13. You call me Teacher and Lord, and rightly so, for that is what I am. 14. Now that I, your Lord and Teacher, have washed your feet, you also should wash one another's feet. 15. I have set you an example that you should do as I have done for you. 16. Very truly I tell you, no servant is greater than his master, nor is a messenger greater than the one who sent him. 17. Now that you know these things, you will be blessed if you do them.'" You may not think of Christ as having a particular leadership style, but clearly, he did. His leadership style is one that I would recommend to every leader to incorporate into their own. Jesus had both power and authority, but He did not feel compelled to assert His deity. He chose to live among sinners, live a life of scorn and ridicule, and ultimately, He gave His life on the cross to spare others. In the following passages of scripture, Christ himself refers to His character as one of a servant:

Mark 10:45 (KJV) For even the Son of man came not to be ministered unto, but to minister, and to give his life as a ransom for many.

John 6:38 (KJV) For I came down from heaven, not to do mine own will, but the will of him that sent me.

Luke 22:27 (KJV) For who is greater, he that sitteth at meat, or he that serveth? Is not he that sitteth at meat? ...I am among you as he that serveth.

Take a moment and reflect on those scripture verses. Think about the behaviors of the leaders within your organization. Or, better yet, think about yourself! How do you measure up in that department? Are you willing to serve others? Are there some people that you think you are above serving? Are you eager to make strategic self-serving connections, purposefully befriending those who can potentially propel you forward? And are you continuously looking to connect with others who can help increase your personal gain? Are you the leader that is always wanting to be elevated, praised or promoted? And do you feel offended if others fail recognize your position of authority? Does your "what is in it for me" attitude get in the way and determine your every move? Or, are you looking for ways to help and serve others for the greater good? Are you humble and confident of the importance of your work and why it has to be done? And will you work conscientiously without any special recognition or praise expected in return? These questions, if answered honestly, will help you identify how close you are to Leading God's Way. Or, how far.

The beautiful thing about true authority is that it affords you the freedom to lead with love and not by force. Many leaders use power and coercion instead of reasoned persuasion. In my opinion, they fail to show compassion and love erroneously fearing that it will be interpreted as a weakness and usurp their authority. Watchman Nee wrote, "If we honor the authority of the Lord in our lives others will respect the Lord's authority in us." Who will choose to lead like Christ?

It will take both confidence and competence to lead God's Way. I challenge you to make a conscious decision to lead His way? Leaders who practice the servant leadership style become skilled in utilizing this power-sharing model of authority. They become adept vision casters and are able to accurately prioritize the needs of their team. These leaders also recognize the importance of getting others to buy-in to their ideas and processes. These leaders can frequently be found encouraging collective decision-making among their team members. "The Best Leaders Are Humble Leaders" is a leadership article written by Jeanine Prime and Elizabeth Salib (MAY 12, 2014) in the Harvard Business Review. This article uses a quote by Google's SVP of People Operations, Lazlo Bock, which states, "Your end goal is what can we do together to problem-solve." This statement by Lazlo about leadership reminded me of an old Chinese Proverb that I love, "Many hands make light work." When we unite for a common cause or task, our desired end-result can be reached more expeditiously.

A faithful servant leader is also a transformative leader who understands that the collective can do more together than one individual working alone. They realize that people do "best" when it is something they want to do. So, it is the leader's responsibility to inspire others to want what they want. This should not be confused with manipulation. This is simply effectively sharing your vision and views in a manner that has the ability to persuade others through validity and merit. People want to see a benefit from their efforts.

Exercise 1: You are interviewing a top candidate to fill a position in your organization and are competing with other companies in your area that can pay more. Hiring this person would be a big win.

What might you say to them, based on the information below, that will convince them that your offer is in their best interest?

General Knowledge Needed for Response: Great leaders possess discernment, and somehow, they seem to instinctively know when it's time to give others the necessary room to grow. Essentially, it is all about equipping and empowering others and giving them the creative space, they need to optimize their abilities. Once individuals get the freedom to embrace where they are, time to develop and trust their abilities, and the opportunities to practice, their confidence grows.

Possible Answer: You have an excellent resume and our organization value people with your skill and ability. We can offer you mentoring, additional training and leadership opportunities to prepare you for future promotions.

General Knowledge Needed for Response: A servant leader must continue to grow themselves. These leaders are making room for others to move into their positions as they begin to transition into higher levels. These confident, mature leaders will not withhold pertinent information to ensure that they alone are in the know. These leaders will not feel challenged or threatened as other members on their team begin to rise in knowledge and skill. In fact, they will feel a sense of pride knowing that their leadership has helped others grow.

Possible Answer: We are always looking for talent within our organization to promote when openings become available. We take great pride in preparing our future leaders.

General Knowledge Needed for Response: A Servant leader instinctively creates environments of inclusion, environments where people experience a sense of unity. If there are noted differences, they will feel a sense of uniqueness and not one of exclusion. According to research by Catalyst, when team members feel more included in the daily operation of the organization, they are more innovative, have higher levels of engagement, and demonstrate more positive citizenship behaviors. This environment makes team members more apt to go above and beyond the "call of duty" to help others meet workgroup objectives.

Possible Answer: It has always been important in this organization to establish of culture of inclusiveness. Anyone working here is more than an employee, they are a valued member of our team.

Abraham Maslow, one of the most influential American psychologists in the 20ᵗʰ century, established Maslow's Hierarchies of Needs. This chart states that all people desire a sense of belonging. A report by Catalyst supports Maslow's Theory noting that when employees feel a sense of belonging they will want to contribute more. Catalyst has also described this style as altruistic leadership and indicates that it can improve diversity and be a morale booster. There is also a downside to any form of leadership style. Servant leaders may be seen as lacking authority at times and can suffer from a conflict of interest. They may be torn between what is good for the employees vs. the organizations' goals. These leaders may put their employees' best interest ahead of the business objectives which causes them to conflict with the organizations' goals. For example, the company's primary interest may be the bottom line of profit. Whereas, a servant leader may advocate offering health insurance for the employees which may decrease the overall net worth and investment viability of the organization. Or, a servant leader may strictly adhere to the organizational goals and directives and suffer from internal conflict because it clashes with their CORE values.

Autocratic Leadership - You can easily recognize this leadership style. These leaders tend to have dominant personalities and hold significant control over staff. This leader may rarely consider a worker's suggestions as having any validity and seldom shares their power. The autocratic leader can be decisive, move ahead and get the job done effectively, but can leave staff feeling restricted and controlled. Unfortunately, this can lead to frustration, stifled creativity, high absenteeism, and a high turnover rate for those under this type of leadership. Also, lower productivity may result from the hesitation made by those on the team who are afraid of making independent decisions even decisions that fall within the scope of their job assignment. These are members who fear reprimand and may develop the tendency to wait for validation or a clear directive to act before proceeding. This often causes undue stress and certainly does not foster loyalty or productivity effectiveness. Nonetheless, this leadership style works well in certain environments where jobs may be mundane, required skill is limited, and where workers can be replaced quickly. It may also be effective in military or governmental agencies where accuracy in replication and consistency is valued over independence and creativity and where questions to the established protocol are unwelcomed.

Laissez-faire Leadership - (laissez-faire means "let them do" in French), leaders with this leadership style are known for their hands-off approach, which allows employees a certain amount of leeway. This leader is extremely effective for those with creative jobs or in workplaces with skilled, experienced personnel. Employees usually handle tasks in a manner they choose as appropriate, within reason. Don't become alarmed; this is not just a free for all. Typically, specific parameters have already been established as a standard by the leader who steps back while the work is being done. Caution: regardless of your leadership style, it is essential to monitor performance routinely and effectively communicate your expectations. This will prevent work standards from slipping and negatively reflecting on your leadership.

Democratic Leadership or Participative Leadership is a style that means leaders will seek the opinions of their team members before making a decision. Workers in this environment usually feel a higher level of job satisfaction because they feel valued and that their opinions matter. One noted drawback to this process is that it is much slower than the autocratic leadership style. This model requires time to gather input from others and additional time to form an agreement on the course of action that should be taken. This style is not the most appropriate in environments where immediate decisions are demanded.

> Note: In an emergency situation, an excellent democratic or participative type leader will recognize the need to temporary change models and can do so effectively.

Bureaucratic Leadership models are seen in all governmental organizations and can be seen in other highly regulated administrative environments. This model ensures accountability and strict adherence to governing laws and rules of operation. Leaders under this model are vigilant as it relates to monitoring others to ensure that the rules and procedures follow the prescribed manner. This works exceptionally well but can stifle innovation and creativity in more innovative and fast-paced organizations.

Charismatic Leadership – This model represents a leader with a robust, energetic personality. This leader has many similarities with the transformational leader. Both styles depend heavily on their persuasive power and charm to influence. This particular leadership style is often viewed less favorably. Why? Although this style is similar to the transformational leader, one of the major downfalls of this style is that in the absence of the Charismatic Leader, the work slows, the vision fails, and the lack of leadership within the team is evident. This type of leadership does not prepare the team members to rise to the level of the Charismatic Leader. Therefore, the removal of the charismatic leader typically leaves a power vacuum within the organization.

Situational Leadership. This type leader is one who steps up to the task at hand. According to Hersey and Blanchard, in theory, this type of leadership is best. A situational leader may utilize a range of different styles depending upon the circumstances or the existing environment. For example, situational leaders can quickly adopt an autocratic leadership style in a crisis moment and then transition smoothly into a democratic leadership style when discussing other non- emergency issues.

We each have a natural propensity for a particular leadership style. However, there may be times when you must stretch and make a switch to become more effective in particular situation or because of changing group dynamics within the group you are leading. It can be challenging to determine what style is most suitable for where you are. Our personalities, temperament, previous experiences are all factors that affect our leadership style. Therefore, knowing yourself, your bias and the people you are leading is crucial.

CHAPTER 3

Communication: An Essential Element

"Some leaders believe you must have all the answers;
a wise leader knows when to ask the right question."
Daniel M. Cash & William H. Griffith

Good leaders must learn to develop their communication skills. Having good oral and written communication skills is a definite asset to persons in any leadership position. Unfortunately, some leaders see conversations as a one-sided vehicle. They want to speak only to be heard. However, there is so much more to good communication. Communication is a two-way process, it is both the sending and receiving of information. The ability to speak and write is an essential tool every leader should possess. In addition, leaders should also master the art of listening. Listening communicates a level of respect for the speaker and also conveys a standard of care and concern for what is being said. When leaders are attentive to speakers, it sends a message that the leader is genuinely interested in their thoughts.

Leaders are vision casters which means that they must be able to create a clear vision and direction for their team. Goals and objectives must be understood in order to be carried out successfully. A leader's skillful use of concrete language creates vivid memorable imagery. In other words, they help others visualize concepts and ideas. Habakkuk 2:2

says, "And the Lord answered me and said: "Write the vision and make it plain upon tablets, that he may run that readeth it." In communicating their vision, leaders may incorporate a variety of media to ensure their communication is clear. They also establish the methods and measures for accomplishing tasks within the scope of the team's skill set. Good leaders are committed to a habit of excellence and naturally set high expectations for their team. However, use caution. You should set the bar high and have great expectations but don't be over ambitious. If a leader's request is unrealistic and beyond the team's ability, they will soon become frustrated, anxious, demonstrate low morale and dissatisfaction. You will hear it repeated throughout this book, it is important to know your people (imitations, aspirations, etc.). Know what they can and cannot do, learn what they need and what motivates them. Remember, the goal is not to achieve for the sake of bragging rights, it is to inspire others to use their God-given talents as unto the Lord." Simply stated, get them to do their best with what they have.

There have been times on my life when active listening wasn't my strong suit. And even now, I find that I am still a work in progress. Nonetheless, I am committed to improving in this area. However, I must admit that I was taken aback a few years ago when someone first brought it to my attention that I was not a good listener. I could not believe it. Or, maybe I just didn't want to believe it. They told me that I habitually completing their sentences. Was I in denial? What? How dare they say that I wasn't a good listener! After recovering from my state of being offended and when the shock wore off that someone actually thought I was not the good listener I thought I was, I began to take notice. I had to stop and reflect.

> Note: You may not like it but if someone reveals something about how you are perceived, take time to reflect. What are you doing to cause that perception?

Just because I thought I was a good listener didn't mean I was. I began thinking of all the times I spent listening to others. Although, I did spend much time listening, there were many times when I was impatient. I started noticing that I did sometimes finish sentences of others. You know, when I thought they were too slow getting to the point. Yes, when I thought I knew where they were heading in the conversation, and thought I could help them get there faster, I was indeed guilty as charged. So, when you learn new information, take a closer look and if you see the error of your ways, please don't ignore it. Act on it and make a change for the better. We all have room for improvement. Start listening to those around you; they might have what you need to hear so that you can become a better leader. Remember, listening shows a level of respect and people deserve the opportunity to complete their thoughts.

Being a good listener also requires that you focus on the speaker and be present in the moment. What does being present in the moment mean? It means that you are attentive to the speaker and not thinking about other things. Being present means you not only are listening to every word that is being said but you are listening for how it is being said and for those subconscious nonverbal cues given. You are noticing the tone and pace of their speech along with their body language. Being present requires active listening. Are you ever guilty of wanting to be prepared with a "great" answer, some thought-provoking response, so much so that you are running ahead of what the speaker is saying so you will have time to compose your response? If you are having to do that, you are doing too much and not giving the speaker the attention they deserve. Strive to improve our listening skills so your answers will be derived organically from what is said. You will find that you will gain more insight into what is being said, insight on some things that may have been omitted. Being a good listener is an essential tool. In good communication. When you are present in the moment you cannot be anxiously anticipating their next statement so that you can have a prepared response ready. It takes discipline to develop listening skills, but you will become a better communicator if you do.

Leaders must be adept in providing quality feedback. Regular feedback equips teams with valuable information and tells them whether they are or are not measuring up to the expectations of their leader. If they are in error, teams will learn what they are doing wrong and can work towards correcting the issue. This is just one of the many reasons timely feedback is crucial. If the feedback is positive, they can move forward with increased confidence in their ability. Failure to do so may exacerbate the waste of materials and time. There is an old saying that you should monitor what you value. Therefore, when you give an assignment, it is not considered micromanaging to check on its progress routinely. Also, it is important to note that immediate praise or criticism has more impact than delayed feedback. This is a simple fact and may sound elementary, but it is one that is often overlooked. Many leaders may rarely acknowledge and praise good work, or they wait until much later. Then when they mention it, it seems like an afterthought. Something to remember is that everyone wants and needs a little praise. Don't just praise the top performer and criticize the lowest performer. Find a way to recognize others who are meeting the expectations although they may not be a shining star.

There is a knack to constructive criticism. If not handled correctly, people become defensive and may harbor resentment when critiqued. This will only further impede their movement toward positive change. An open-ended questioning method that coaches' employ will help them identify their own areas of improvement. For example, learn to ask essential questions of the person about their performance. Ask them, "If another approach had been taken to the problem, how would that have impacted the outcomes? Or, would the results have been the same?" Allow them time to process and explain their reasoning. Questions similar to these will prompt them to identify their own mistakes and ultimately make them more accountable for improving. It also reduces the probability of any ill will towards you, because their dignity would still be intact. Why? Because you didn't tell them where they performed poorly and failed, instead, you empowered them to identify problems and find solutions themselves. This strategy helps ensure lasting change and growth of those that you lead. As you work more towards implementing coaching questioning strategies and using positive reinforcements for things done well. It will become easier to you. Thus, helping you keep the focus on the desired behaviors and not the negative ones.

Jesus mastered using questioning throughout His ministry, as a means of teaching. In Matthew 12:10-11, Jesus is asked is it lawful to heal on the Sabbath? His response was to ask a reflective question, "If any of you has a sheep and it falls into a pit on the Sabbath, will you not take hold of it and lift it out?" Skillful use of questioning can guide people from where they want to be to where they need to be. Good coaching questions are usually open-ended, thought-provoking, and will elicit a deeper level of thought for the response. Jesus was a master of this type of questioning. It causes a person to listen, reflect, respond, and grow as a means of leading. In Matthew 16:15, He says, "Who do you say that I am?" Peter's response, "You are the Christ, the Son of the Living God." Peter's answer would dictate his future direction. If he believed what he said, and he did, then his future actions would reflect it. When you get followers to reflect on what is real and vital, their future actions will also reflect it.

Remember, effective leaders deliver constructive feedback with specificity. If the leader is unclear, his message can easily be misunderstood or misinterpreted. Typically, when this happens, there is no improvement and the listener will be confused and may or may not ask for clarity which is unfortunate. If listeners fail to ask for clarity, it may be because of their rapport with leaders. They may feel unsafe expressing their lack of understanding, not wanting to appear inept. Subsequently, they continue with their mediocre performance when better communication could have remedied the situation. There are some who choose not to ask for clarity and even worse, they dismiss all that they did not understand as being unimportant.

Leaders must stress the importance of how specific actions will affect the team or the organization. Be clear when you tell members how you feel. Let them know how their singular actions impact others. Don't assume they know. Remember, whenever possible, use "I feel" statements when addressing your team. "I feel..." statements are not accusatorial and are interpreted as less threating which lessens defensive attitudes some team members may be prone to get. Take a moment to reflect on the scripture, "do unto others as you would have them do unto you." How would you like someone to speak to or about you? Last but not least, end on a high note. Think of something positive to end your feedback. There is always something positive even if it is only to say, "I have confidence in our team and know we can do much better." This softens the blow and makes your words of criticism more palatable. Remember, the whole purpose of constructive criticism is to communicate ways to make things better. If your delivery is such that anger is the result felt by your team, much of your feedback may be rejected, and your main point lost. So, be mindful should you choose not to conclude with a positive statement. Thoughts to remember:

1. The likelihood of your feedback achieving its desired purpose is slim if you fail to end on a positive note.
2. Always express your confidence in the team's ability to improve.
3. Beneficial feedback must be timely and clear. It should describe what future improvements will look like and ways they might be achieved.
4. Express appreciation of all effort exerted to make the needed changes.

We have all heard the adage, "if you don't have something nice to say, don't say anything at all." I recall hearing that more times than I care to recount as a youth. However, is that really good advice for a leader? It sounds good and may work sometime, but unfortunately, leaders are not afforded this luxury. Good leaders are responsive and must address the truth. The truth is not always pleasant. Sometimes it may be Good but there will be many times when it's Bad or Ugly. Nonetheless, thoughtful delivery by the leader is a must. Learn to speak the truth in love and look for something good to say. Even the smallest positive can make the biggest difference during stressful situations.

According to Tine Thygesen, a contributing writer for Forbes, one of the most important and underrated disciplines a person can have is leadership skills. I must agree, I have seen people go into leadership positions with little or no formal leadership training. Some did very well but there were others who suffered. Often, the training received after securing a leadership position is minimal. This is problematic and can make it difficult for new leaders to adjust quickly and thrive in their new roles. For new hires, there is always a learning curve with any new position and there will. always be an adjustment period. For example, when people have little or no leadership experience the internal emotional stress of the adjustment they experience is compounded. In addition, their lack of preparedness is evidenced in the absence of guidance they are able to offer to those working on assignments appointed to them. Subsequently, there is a high possibility of productivity loss during this adjustment period. All of these factors impact the organizations daily operation.

Some people seemingly have an inherent ability to lead others. You see this all the time. Nonetheless, everyone can learn basic strategies and begin developing characteristics that help them grow into better leaders. There are a vast number of leadership styles, and leaders will vary in the degree in which they incorporate the different styles. Knowing all styles and being able to integrate them when needed can be useful. The mere fact that you have chosen to read this book says that you are interested in growing as a leader and desire to lead God's way. What does leading God's way intel? It is about helping people achieve their highest potential through your servant leadership. To be a servant leader means that you are committed to meeting people where they are and empowering them to move forward. It also says that you are committed to the process and the mission, continually working to strengthen the organization while building and supporting people you are supervising. It's about helping others see their value and inspiring them to do their best. One of the characteristics of servant leaders is that they can be trusted. Their authenticity is felt by those working with them and for them. We know that accepting any leadership role in any capacity can be a challenge, but with it also comes rewards.

In my lifetime, I have been fortunate to have been surrounded by leaders who inspire me to aspire. One of whom is my pastor, Bishop Fullwood, who often says, "Preparation is never a waste of time!" This subtle reminder lets us know that we should be proactive and must always be willing to prepare ourselves for future opportunities. We should not become complacent and expect good things to come our way without any effort. We prepare by developing our craft, and by continuing to learn; but also, by preparing mentally. As we deepen our relationship with God, our expectation level, faith and confidence in Him helping us succeed rises. Mental preparedness is when you believe it can be accomplished and can visualize being successful,\. You must be able to see in faith and speak in confidence.

Leaders must acknowledge the fact that occasionally there will be times when they may have to stand alone in the face of opposition. At those times, they will need to have the confidence and faith to stand boldly on their beliefs and their trust in God for a positive outcome. And they must also use caution and rely on what is factual and not act on feelings alone generated from the emotions that may be attached to the situation. Have you ever heard this old saying, "you have to get your head in the game?" I have heard of this phrase associated with sports. I believe it also applies as it relates leadership. To be both compelling and believable, you must first see yourself as a leader. Believe that you possess the ability and intellect to do the job, then stay focused and determined with an expectation of good results. This in no way means that you know it all. Leaders will never know everything but will become expert in utilizing their vast resources. They use outside sources for additional training to learn the mechanics of leading such as goal setting, budgeting, marketing, or whatever areas apply to their particular company or organization. Good leaders are lifelong learners and continue to grow.

Don't let doubt and personal insecurities rob you of your ability to move forward. Understandably, there may be days when you have demons of doubt questioning your ability to lead. There may be times when a well-thought-out plan or project flops. That's life! You are not the only one who has faced disappointments. When you accept that fact that you will not be successful every time and that there will be disappointments in your life, you are already ahead of the game. Your response is to put your trust in God, ask for wisdom as you do your due diligence, plan carefully, look at possible barriers, and then look for ways to mitigate any potential disappointments. Hopefully, those feelings of doubt will be short-lived and not occur daily.

Leaders may experience isolation or loneliness. These feelings can be experienced by a leader who has made an unpopular decision. New leaders or very social leaders may be more susceptible to this feeling of isolation than an experienced or autocratic leader. Regardless of your leadership type, there will be days when you feel that you are isolated and alone with no one or only a few with whom to share your concerns. You may often feel a lack of respect and that your authority is threatened, but in spite of that, leaders push through and understand that leadership has its price. All leaders, at some point, will experience a varying degree of doubt and insecurities, but those doubts cannot be allowed to stay at the forefront of their minds. This is the time when a leader's knowledge of people and having excellent interpersonal skills is invaluable. It will help them navigate through this time of isolation.

Leaders with a fixed mindset have more difficulty than those with a growth mindset when it comes to accepting challenges and innovative learning. When things go wrong, leaders with a fixed mindset start believing that they are inadequate merely because they cannot do a particular job. They allow one setback to define them forever. This attitude is unhealthy for anyone but especially those in leadership roles. Leaders with a fixed mindset may also cover up what they don't know and feel threatened by others who easily grasp concepts they find difficult. Carol Dweck (2012) found that people with a fixed mindset believed that their abilities and intelligence were inherently fixed. When you have a fixed mindset, you want to appear smart at all times, thereby avoiding difficult challenges. Fixed mindset people often shy away from potential growth opportunities and are highly sensitive to being wrong. Whereas, those with a growth mindset find that although they may have a learning curve, and there are some areas where they lack proficiency, they are confident that they possess the ability to grow and develop. A leader with a growth mindset welcomes new learning, and they are often eager to explore methods or techniques that may stretch their current skill level and performance. Their confidence and esteem remain in tack as they step up to the challenge and continue to thrive. Yeager & Dweck's research indicated that intellectual ability alone was not the determining factor to success in the students studied. They found that a growth mindset was a critical element of their success. Once again, another nod to scripture being manifested in our daily lives; Proverbs 23:7, "For as a man thinketh in his heart so is he…"

One thing you must remind yourself of as a leader is that whenever you assume a new position, it is just that, a new position. There will be an adjustment period, and there will be many things that you will not know. Be kind to yourself, anyone else stepping into the new job would feel similar emotions. This feeling of anxiousness is because you want to do a good job. Don't be afraid to seek help as you find your way through. Also, continue seeking God on how to work in this new position. You will want to align yourself with people who can support you in your leadership role. Do you know anyone that will be an excellent mentor to you? Who is a person that you can depend on giving you honest feedback? Honest feedback will help you to develop and to grow. Contrary to what some leaders would have you believe; no leader has ever known it all or will know it all. So, stop holding yourself to that level and be gracious to yourself when you err. Although you will never know it all, you can commit to becoming a lifelong learner, and connect with people and resources that can provide the information you will need to solve problems as they arise.

There will be times, as vacancies become available, that a new leader may be chosen from within the organization's team. This leader will go through an adjustment period in this new role should be aware of any subtle changes in the rapport between other team members. This is not at all unusual and healthy relationships can be retained. However, there may be a need to establish boundaries or redefining acceptable interaction. Recognizing the new relationship dynamics will make it easier for you and those working with you. This shift in leadership dynamics means you are no longer waiting to receive instructions, directives, and orders, but you are now the person giving, coaching, delegating, encouraging, and motivating.

The delegation of duties comes more naturally to some than it does for others. For example, I am a hands-on kind of person and must remind myself of the importance of enlisting others and delegating. Delegation is particularly tricky for me when it is a special project, or some may call it "my baby!" For me, this continues to be an area of growth. And I have said it before, I am a work in progress. Remember, self-awareness is key and acknowledging area/s of weakness is the beginning of excellence. When you have more than one person, it takes a team effort to operate at optimum performance and good leaders learn to share the load. Identify the people who can do what you need, enlist their help, give clear assignments, and then follow up. Also, make sure you understand that follow-up- is not the same as micro-managing. Trust those you have selected to do the job assigned. Initially, your time spent explaining, setting up timelines and clarifying expected outcomes may seem laborious. However, it is time upfront will be to your benefit. Once they understand your vision and expectations, they can carry them out to your satisfaction, yielding you great results.

Leaders want to create an environment that is conducive to others producing the optimal outcome. Talented people must have the space to do it and they will thrive on this autonomy within the scope of their job. How are you encouraging growth with your team? I have learned over the years; there is a definite difference between assigning a task and assigning responsibility. Great leaders assign responsibilities. What is the difference? Delegation means that you have designated a job to a person along with giving them a certain level of decision-making authority. Assigning a task limits creativity and reduces accountability. A person assigned to a task is responsible for the function and has no delegated decision-making authority unless specifically given that authority. Leaders should know their **CORE VALUES,** have good moral standards and be able to resist offers that compromise their integrity. If you think an opportunity is too good to be true, it probably is. Although leaders must frequently make quick decisions, they should always take the needed time to look at the big picture. When opportunities look too good, the promising attractiveness that draws you in may be a disguise to future costly outcomes. If you don't already know and if you do not have ample time to acquire the needed information for an informed decision, ask for more time to gather pertinent facts. Leaders know the cost of acting hastily. Learn to say "yes or no" with authority when it is your best answer.

Years ago, while employed as a school administrator, a colleague and I were looking for ways to inspire students never to give up. We brainstormed for a while and came up with the *acronym* FOCUS (Fearlessly Optimize Challenges Until Success). This acronym would be a reminder to students when preparing for and during the End-Of-Grade testing to stay the course and be positive. Leaders also benefit from reminders when experiencing difficult times. Reminders to channel energies, focus, and persist, can be the needed boost to propel you forward through challenging situations. Mediocrity should not be the acceptable standard simply because things get tough. FOCUS and continue striving for excellence.

Leaders need a sense of organization and should not operate out of chaos. When organized, tasks are handled efficiently, and valuable time is not lost needlessly processing paperwork. Better yet, valuable time will not be spent trying to find misplaced documents. Excellent organizational skills will prove to reduce stress and elevate the confidence others place in you. Organizational skills and time management are vital components to balancing your life. Good leaders are proactive with the keen ability to anticipate barriers to their goals. Not only can they foresee problems, but they possess the intellect and creative talent to formulate solutions. Organization is a requirement as it may become difficult for some people to stay on course because of the many things they have to do. However, an astute leader fully understands that distractions will hinder their progress and remain vigilant. They are purposeful in their activities ensuring that all align towards achieving the desired end goal.

An effective leader is both responsible and responsive. This leader skillfully guides the organization towards its primary objective or mission, yet, it is always open to accepting ideas from others and will look for opportunities to incorporate them. This type leader encourages and fosters creativity and establishes an atmosphere of trust where workers feel inspired to generate new ideas that may expedite and bring your goals into fruition. This same atmosphere will allow you to let them know when their views conflict with the goals you have. As the leader, you thank them for their suggestions for the project but let them know that this is not something you will be doing. Of course, you will want to do it in a manner that will keep the door open for future ideas and continued loyalty to your leadership.

Understand your leadership role. Don't be afraid to have employees disagree with you. They don't need to agree with you in all situations, but they do need to respect you and be confident in your guidance. Your track record of previous achievements will garner their respect and trust. Those who follow you need to know that they can be open and honest with you at all times. It is to your benefit to be open and honest with them in return. Warning: there is a certain level of patience that is needed here. Be considerate of the fact that everyone has not been privy to all of the information that you have. Therefore, be prepared to restate, reframe, and reiterate your statements, until they are clearly understood. It is also equally important for you to listen to them for understanding. Learn how to talk to your people. Know where they are in their maturity level, mental acuity, emotionally, intellectually, and relatability. Develop the eye of an eagle and become very observant. Take note of social cues that may give insight into how the conversation is going. Understand the importance of slight changes in speech and movements. Know what is in the best interest of not only the organization but the people who are in it. It is essential to have the courage of a lion to forge ahead during challenging times. You must be courageous to stand for what you believe or to exact disciplinary measures.

When leading God's way, you must be willing to follow through and not accept the easiest or the path most frequently traveled. You will not always be understood by those you lead and may often feel isolated or even ostracized. When you are feeling unpopular, you must tap into your inner strength and resolve to act in a manner that is still in alignment with your primary objective; yes, do this while being compassionate, caring, and understanding of those who don't understand you. That is a tall order but is the requirement. Leading God's way requires that you be willing to invest time, energy, and thoughtfulness, into other people. One important note here: being responsible for large numbers does not equate to success. It is doing what God has called you to do. So, whether you have a few people or thousands under your leadership, seek to know and do what God has called you to do. Then, you will see be successful.

Flattery in and of itself has little value and trivializes your compliments. Most people can detect when you are insincere. They can tell when you are interested and doing things from the heart or when you are just flattering. In my opinion, being honest with compassionate delivery always trumps over saying something just because it sounds good. Leaders whose actions are opposed to what they say is like reading FAKE News! If you are trying to be nice and purposely withhold the brutal truth, your dishonesty is doing them a disservice. "Certainly, constructive criticism can be helpful. An insightful point of light presented by someone who truly has your best interests at heart can illuminate an area where you need to improve." (Joel Olsten, becoming a Better You page 229). The growth of those that follow you is limited when you provide inadequate or unclear feedback. You may be unwittingly fostering unwarranted stress on them with the lack of or vague directives. Your actions may ultimately cause a slow-down in productivity and increase the overall expense of the organization.

There is no need to assert your position or make it a point to remind others that you have a higher position of authority over them. Retain your humility. When leaders feel they must remind others of their authority, they have a position and are not genuinely operating as a leader. Leaders that are good at their jobs don't have to flaunt their power or laud it for it to be recognized. They will never have to tell others that they are leaders. Their history stands as a testimony of their leadership ability, power, and authority. Furthermore, their character and integrity generate influence, which is indicative of their leadership.

Full-time office workers average over 8.8 hours a day, according to the Bureau of Labor Statistics. A study of approximately 2,000 office workers indicated that a majority of those people were not highly productive for those 8.8 hours. In essence, employers are paying employees for time spent web surfing, checking social media, engaging in non-work-related conversations with co-workers, smoking breaks, and a sundry of other time-consuming activities. As with any research, extremes are averaged into the totals. Some people routinely misuse office freedoms while others with a higher work ethic will waste less time. I was amazed at the low number of productive hours in a day. They estimate that the average worker produces productively for three hours. So, now that we understand that workers are not always going to work at their peak performance and will not be highly productive 100% of their time, our goal is to have them proficiently operating when they are working. The hope is to get your team to exceed the reported 3-hour average. Leaders valuing high productivity must monitor what they value and always be cognizant of changes that may affect it. They may also implement some flexibility if warranted. A demanding leader lacking compassion may cause even the best workers to burn out or quit. Remember, the best leaders are ones who appreciate and respect the individuals that work for them. They have learned to praise the work and contributions of those helping them attain their goals.

Constantly working under stress is unhealthy and impairs your decision-making ability. According to research, "One of the primary targets of stress hormones is prefrontal cortex (McEwen, 2007), a region controlling high level "executive" functions including working memory, inhibition of distraction, novelty-seeking, and decision making (Miller, 1999; Stuss and Knight, 2002)." I highly recommend that find a person or persons that you trust and allow them to become your support group.

A support group provides you with opportunities to share personal experiences and feelings in a safe, non-threatening environment. Everyone needs to have a support group, and you are no different. With this group, you will be able to discuss various topics and receive coping strategies and other pertinent information that will benefit you. And know that you are not alone in the struggle. Numerous research studies have proved that a support system has many positive benefits, such as higher levels of well-being, better coping skills, and longer, healthier life. Studies also show that social support can cause a reduction in stress, depression, and anxiety.

CHAPTER 4

*T*ransparency: *M*odel *C*haracter

Good leaders...invest their time, energy, money,
and thinking, into growing others as leaders.
John Maxwell

Building Character. Character is often defined by what is done rather than what is said. Every decision we make affects how the world views us. Our choices show the world a glimpse of our real character. Leading an organization with integrity and good character can, at times, have a negative financial impact on the bottom line. This can be true in our personal lives, too. There will be times when doing the right thing will cost us, but, maintaining your integrity is well worth it. It is times like these that character sets us apart. When your goal is to live consistently in a manner that models ethical behavior, your conscious will be a reminder when you veer off course. Listen to it and don't try to override it. Trust its voice; it will pay off in the end. So, even if you suffer temporarily because of your ethical decision, you will ultimately gain inner peace. And though the prospects of recognition from others did not drive your moral action, others will learn of it and respect you for your integrity. You will have contributed to making the world a better place. Isaiah 32:17 says, "The fruit of that righteousness will be peace; its effect will be quietness and confidence forever." Similarly, Philippians 4:13 tells us, "I can do all this through him who gives me strength." To make any significant change, one must first realize that there is a need to change; being self-aware is critical.

What are the indicators that change is needed? Change is necessary when goals are not being met when you are no longer current (this also includes technological innovations), and if the personnel turnover rates are high. **You must believe in yourself and trust the process.** What happens when you don't think change is possible for you? One thing that happens is that you give up, you don't try because you feel that your efforts are futile. When you don't believe change is possible for you, you lose hope.

Build up your self-esteem. One necessary element of any leader is to have a healthy dose of self-confidence. Too often we look for external affirmation. When we continuously seek to be affirmed by others, we leave ourselves open and vulnerable. When this affirmation is absent, we are left doubting our self-worth and ability. There are ways to increase self-esteem. Good leaders will develop an internal source of affirmation. They understand the importance of building up their self-confidence. They know that they have the techniques and the power to do so. It's all about you. It is all in the way you think. You choose how you view yourself and how you want others to see you. It's up to you to change your limited belief system.

a). There are enough external critics, and their negative thoughts about us are outside of our sphere of control. However, we do have control over what we think so we must shut down our inner critic.

b). When things are going badly, and they sometimes will take a minute to find one thing that you are doing well. Focus on it and give yourself an appreciation break. You deserve it!

c). Get in a daily habit of listing at least three things that you are proud of and appreciate about yourself and write them down. It may sound silly, but it works.

d). Do the right thing! When you do the right thing, you are not burdened with unnecessary guilt.

e). Replace the perfectionism. Some people find it difficult to do anything because they want it to be perfect. That is not how life works. Good leaders are cognizant of their decisions and how they may impact their lives and others. Therefore, they commit to doing their due diligence before making decisions. They are willing to lead even at risk of being imperfect. There is a quote by Sarah Ban

Breathnach that I like, which says, "the world needs dreamers, and the world needs doers, but above all, the world needs dreamers that will do." What that means to me is that dreamers dream for perfection while good leaders work perfecting the dream. They are willing to try and believe that they can accomplish their goals. It is essential to put yourself in an environment that promotes change. It is equally important to be surrounded by people who believe in you and have information and skills that will help you achieve.

Recognize confidence drainers in your life. Low self-awareness of surroundings, work, home, relationships, life changes, and one's thoughts or beliefs are problematic. Rehashing unfavorable events of the past can be depressing and hold you captive. Choose not to be a victim. Minimizing your contributions, jumping to negative conclusions, and negative self-talk, can drain your life of positive self-esteem and inspiration. Leaders must be aware of the power of negative thoughts and not to succumb to them.

Follow the Golden Rule. Do unto others as you would have them do unto you. It would help if you also were compassionate toward others. The Bible tells us in 1 Corinthians 13 that, "love is kind." In other words, it looks for ways to help people improve their lives. Good leaders should strive to be charitable. A leader must be quick to accurately assess what is occurring in and around him or her; this is crucial. Be familiar with what is causing you to feel and act in a particular way. Identify whether they are factors at work, personnel, personal relationship concerns, or life changes. A leader's thoughts and belief systems will impact their decisions. Therefore, it is essential that they acknowledge what they are. We are what we think we are; so, pay close attention to what we allow our minds to dwell on. Our thoughts have a powerful impact on what we do in life. Are you usually a cynical and pessimistic person? Do you often doubt your ability to accomplish important goals? Is your self-talk harmful? To develop and maintain healthy self-esteem, it is imperative that you understand the power of your inner voice and your thoughts.

God created everyone with free will. We all must make our own decisions. The decision to become a better you is yours. To make any change requires effort on your part and we know change is difficult. It requires discipline to eliminate bad habits and create new ones. Our current practices create our future, so, be willing to take a self-assessment. It is when we take inventory of our lives that we can see areas that need change. Becoming better forces, us to take an honest look at who we are and how we relate and react to others.

Are there some things you know you need to get under control? Perhaps, your words can sound sharp in your responses. Do you react before hearing all of the details? When things go wrong, are you quick to take it as a personal affront and retaliate? Do you harbor ill will and hold onto the past, unwilling to resolve it and let it go? Are you quick to enlist others to join forces against others who disagree with your personal opinion? Or, do you continue sharing your vision, inviting others to join your cause without animosity? Do you have the ability to meet others where they are and provide instruction, training, resources, and support, to help them grow and maximize their potential? There is no one perfect leader, but our Lord, so we are not expected to be perfect in every area. However, it should be our heart's desire to become more like Him. By choosing to read this book, you have shown that you are willing to look inwardly and identify areas of needed growth. One day at a time, your commitment to change will move you closer to "Leading God's Way.

10 Confidence Boosters

1 Focus. Identify the skill you need to acquire. Find out how you can gain it an begin your incremental process to do so.	**6 Be Consistent.** Remind yourself that you don't have to be perfect, but you do have to be consistent. Consistently practicing builds up your confidence. Why? because as you practice, you will see improvement.
2 Prepare. Preparation and practice are essential to having confidence. Preparation requires discipline and consistency.	**7 Manage Fear.** When fear cripples you, you are unable to think clearly or perform at your best. Stay resilient, keep the faith, and develop the "I Can Spirit!"
3 Monitor self-talk. Be positive and eliminate negative, self-limiting words about yourself from your vocabulary. They can sabotage your confidence.	**8 Speak affirmations.** Write down a few words, a positive statement or a slogan that you can repeat regularly. These will build your confidence up.
4 Listen to Music. Music has a psychological effect on your mood. Create an inspiring, uplifting playlist to enjoy when you need a confidence booster.	**9 Believe in Yourself.** Dare to dream and believe in it. Know that there is GREATness in you and that you have something to offer.
5 Get a support team. Know who you can reach out to when you need to brainstorm ideas.	**10 Act.** Even when you are afraid, learn to take small steps forward. These small acts will give you the confidence to take on larger projects. Don't miss opportunities to transform your life. You can do it!!!

If I lead, who will follow me?

Printed with Permission of Author, Dr. Janice Carter Brown

If my sister gets left behind, is the fault mine?
If her dreams collapse and die, at my feet does the blame lie?
If the knowledge that I possess is somehow the best
That I can offer her,
Do I keep it locked inside, tucked away, buried deeper and deeper?
As if I was not my sister's keeper?

If my sister's heart is broken,
Does her pain become a token of what not to allow to happen to me?
Or do I open my own hope chest of pain
So, both our hearts yet remain healed and open
For love to come in again?
If my sister gives up in despair
Will I be there to help repair what's left
Of her ego?

Will her self-esteem be one more lost dream?
Will I follow the golden rule to do unto others
That which I desire to be my lot;
To perpetuate the cycle of strength and tenacity
To share what I've got, never giving up?

For failure is not the lack of success,
Rather failure is never trying to succeed;
Each step, a stepping stone,
Each loss, a win toward the end result.
If my sister gets lost
Will I fear to incur the cost

To travel down that same path, whether of fear, fault or wrath
To find my sister, to restore my sister, to take her hand?
If I lead, who will follow me?

Who will see and understand that I know the way,
That I know what price to pay;

That I Have traveled a road that goes somewhere
A hope of success and accomplishment there?
If I lead who will follow me?
Is my confidence enough for two?
Will it carry me and you?

Dr. Janice Carter Brown, author, Further Along On This Woman's Journey and Dusty Roads, creates timeless and thought-provoking poetry. Although this poem was written specifically for women, any leader can ask themselves this question, "If I Lead Who Will Follow Me?"

Are you the type leader that others will follow?

What does your track record look like?

Does your confidence in your competence reassure others that you can do it?

Do share your knowledge, experiences and setbacks with others to encourage them along the way?

Self-Reflection Questions

1. Is it ever a good idea to risk losing someone's trust for your temporary pleasure or financial gain?

2. What are some examples of this?

3. What would you say to someone to instill the importance of being trustworthy?

4. How important is trust in your relationships with friends and family?

5. Do you think these relationships be negatively affected if you discovered that someone was purposefully lying to you?

6. Would you confront them, let it pass, or would you steam silently?

7. What are some possible outcomes of confrontation?

8. What are possible outcomes if you let it pass?

9. What will be the result if you simply brew quietly?

10. Can you think of other options and consequences?

11. It is a well-known fact that once trust has been broken, it can be challenging to restore. What are some things you can do to earn lost trust?

12. Reflect a moment, have you ever lost someone's trust or has someone lose yours?

13. How difficult was it to re-establish the trust and move forward and are you still suffering from it? Explain.

14. If asked, would your friends and family describe you as trustworthy?

15. Do you find that you are more trustworthy with your family members than friends? If so, why?

16. Do you think your family should trust you automatically?

17. Have you ever taken an unpopular stand and had to pay the price for it with respect to how people viewed you but felt God was pleased with your action?

18. What did you do? What did you learn from the experience?

19. Is it easier to go with the flow than to stand against a commonly accepted practice?

20. Are you willing to take a stand for a cause that is right even if it is unpopular?

21. Have you already done something similar to that? If so, give an example.

22. Whether at home or work, sometimes we are confronted with conflicting views and decisions must be made. What does "compromising your principles" mean to you?

23. If you want someone to trust you, who bears most of the responsibility— you or the other person? Why?

Discussion Questions

Generally, we trust people until they cause us to doubt their honesty and only stop trusting them when they prove unworthy. Some people are overly cautious and skeptical of most people.

1. Explain some possible advantages or disadvantages of being a skeptic.

2. Describe how it feels to be trustworthy and how it may look in those around you.

3. Discuss the long-term benefits of being a trustworthy leader.

4. Think about the noticeable benefits of a trustworthy

    Working community. Then, name at least three ways you benefit from the trustworthiness of others.

1. How we live our lives will dictate how we will be remembered. How do you think you will be remembered?

2. What might people about you when you are gone?

3. What changes are you willing to make to ensure that you will be remembered in a more positive light?

4. What does this saying mean, "your life speaks volumes!"

5. God created each of us with unique gifts. What is your special gift/s?

How are you using them?

If not, why not?

Reflection Questions

Would you compromise your principles to gain the favor of a superior or garner a promotion?

What happens when you make choices that are consistent with your CORE VALUES?

What happens when you make decisions that are inconsistent with your CORE VALUES? How do you feel?

All through the scriptures, we can see the importance of a person's character and integrity. In the world we live in today, we see many immoral things occurring in all areas. It is evident that honesty is often sorely compromised. We know that no one human is faultless and perfection and flawless integrity can only be found in Jesus. Nevertheless, our goal is to strive to be more like Him and through Him. We will then be able to demonstrate integrity for ourselves.

Proverbs 12:22 (KJV)

"Lying lips are an abomination to the LORD: but they that deal truly are his delight."

Confidence is a feeling of certainty and of self-assurance that comes when we appreciate our abilities or qualities. This is not always easy to accomplish. Sometimes we may find it easy to tell others how they should be and yet we have difficulty doing so ourselves. We can even feel guilty when doing things that are in our own best interest. Why? Because we don't fully appreciate our value. Knowing your value will help ensure self-care which is essential to living a balanced life. According to a Mayo Clinic Staff report, low self-esteem can negatively affect every aspect of your life, relationships, job performance, and your physical health.

<u>Confidence boosters:</u>

REFRAMING- is the ability to look at a situation through a different lens, using a different perspective. This often helps solve problems because when you change your perspective it broadens your focus. Reframing may also increase self-esteem. When you are able to look at the negative with a different perspective you may be able to see something positive as a result of your perspective shift. Practice focusing on the positive.

Never forget, WORDS have power and you are accountable for your words. Things are conceptualized in our mind and these thoughts are private until they generate spoken words. Its then that they become contain Words are containers of action. Good Leaders realize they have the ability to enlighten or shift thoughts and beliefs with words. At first thought, do you think this is negative or positive. Good leaders are thoughtful speakers and do not take this ability lightly and use care when speaking to others.

Leaders need tenacity, confidence, and the desire to practice replacing negative or inaccurate thoughts with positive or correct ones. The ability to do this will help reinforce a leader's ability to stay positive. Shifting one's thoughts can be the result of viewing negative situations with a different perspective. The ability to REFRAME an issue can greatly increase a person's problem-solving ability. The essential idea of reframing is that your point-of-view depends on the frame in which it is viewed. It is a way of looking at a challenging situation from all angles, exploring possibilities and seeing them as opportunities rather than a point of defeat.

David was a great leader, yet the scripture notes that he had to encourage himself. Learn how to build up your spirit when things are not favorable. Yes, leaders need to learn how to encourage themselves when things are down. Practice using positive/hopeful statements. Be generous and use kind words when talking about yourself. Celebrate your accomplishments no matter how small and don't hesitate to pat yourself on the back when you know this is only temporary; then, be optimistic and expect things to get better. Understand that negative self-talk will only reinforce feelings of doubt: I am not good enough, I don't look pretty enough, people don't like me, I will never be able this or that. It is important that you think positively.

> Forgive yourself. You are not without flaws nor is anyone else. We all make mistakes — the mistakes can be the beginning of something great when your attitude is right. Can you think of any examples? A mistake that happens today seem devastating but a year from now it may be only a faint memory. Everyone will make mistakes, and most of them can be repaired, fixed, and forgotten. Try not to overreact.

➤ Remove judgmental words about yourself from your thoughts. There are times when we hold ourselves to an unattainable standard. Be aware of this and don't fall into this trap. Try not to use 'should' and 'must' statements. For example, I should have done this, or I must do this. If your thoughts are full of these words, you might be putting unreasonable demands on yourself — or others. Removing these words from your thoughts can lead to more realistic expectations.

➤ Focus on the positive. One excellent way to help you think about the positive is to have a gratitude journal. Daily journaling will allow you to focus on the good that is happening in your life or has happened.

➤ Reflect continually on what you've learned. Everything that we experience can be a lesson. Negative experiences can teach us valuable lessons that will enable us to have a positive outcome should we encounter similar difficulties.

➤ Reframing upsetting thoughts is *essential*. Take time to ask yourself, "What can I do to make the situation less stressful?" Can I see this through another perspective? What good can come out of the situation?

➤ Always remember to encourage yourself. You will not always have a cheerleader in your corner. Learn to be your own cheerleader. When you do something, permit yourself to give yourself credit. For example, I enjoy baking cakes. If one doesn't turn out as I would like, I don't usually fall out and get depressed. I look at it and speak the truth, the cake wasn't pretty, but it was moist and tasty. Reframing says, "I did well. I got two out of three; have a cup of coffee and sit down."

Self-motivation Pointers:

1. Identify troubling conditions or situations. Realize that when we master the art of encouraging ourselves, we will find it easier to inspire others. So trust me, there will be many days when you will need the ability to encourage yourself. I have heard it said that we give what we need most, I am an encourager. I guess in

my lifetime, I needed that and learned how to encourage myself so that I could be used to encourage others.

Again, think about the conditions or situations that seem to play havoc on your self-esteem. Also, if you need to, start singing Donald Lawrence's song, "Encourage Yourself." I love the lyrics, "Sometimes you have to encourage yourself, sometimes you have to speak victory during the test." It goes on to say, "No matter how you feel, speak the word and you will be healed." Speak over YOURSELF. I am taking a Praise Break!

2. Step back from your thoughts and realize that they are merely more or less words and you have the power to choose which words you think about. Learn to control what you think.

3. Accept your thoughts. You must be aware of how powerful your thoughts are. You don't have to like how you are thinking but to deny it is not beneficial. When you acknowledge and recognize how you are thinking you can lessen the power of these thoughts and consequently their influence on your behavior.

4. Embrace and accept your value as a person. As you grow and your self-esteem increases, your confidence and overall sense of well-being will automatically begin to soar. You are of great value, and there is GREATness in you so seize every effort to take care of yourself. This is easier said than done for a busy woman.

5. Take steps to get plenty of rest and be aware that we are what we eat. If you are a fast food and snack food addict, look for ways to reduce empty calories from your diet. I have been working on this for a while and still lack discipline in this area. However, I always say, awareness in one step closer to getting it done. So, there is still hope for me to eat healthier and exercise at least 20-30 minutes a day. So, if you are in the same boat with me, you already know that increasing your consumption of fruits and vegetables will be a plus. Also, there is a need to limit sweets, junk food, and excessive animal fats. Pray for me, and I will pray for you on this disciplined journey to better health.

Christian Leaders demonstrate character in many ways. Look at Matthew 23:11(KJV) "But he that is greatest among you shall be your servant." In Matthew 23:33, why did Jesus rebuke the religious leaders and when He did, and why did it shock them? He called the most regarded and respected leaders of that day snake and vipers. These were the upper echelon, the elite in this ancient community; these were the most educated, they regularly fasted and prayed. Yes, these leaders were commonly known for their piety? Why would Jesus call them vipers? He did so because He knew that they talked a good game because of their knowledge, social acumen, and position. However, they failed to live their lives following their professed religious beliefs.

Leaders committed to leading God's way will read the Word, hear God's Word and apply it to their lives. Romans 10:17 (NKJV) says, "so then, faith comes by hearing, and hearing by the word of God." If no one had ever told me about Jesus and God's plan for my life, or if I had never read for myself about Him, I would be clueless about the need for faith.

1. **Read the Word** - Reading or hearing God's Word is like planting a garden. If you want to grow or "build" a garden, you must first plant the seeds, or the actual plant or flower. God's Word is the seed that grows the faith. Knowing His promises, what God says about you, about life, and about Jesus' plan for eternal life, won't transplant into your brain by osmosis. Become familiar with the Bible and what faith is all about by meditating on its contents. This will give you the basis for growing or increasing your faith.

2. **Heed the Word** - James 1:22-24(NKJV) offers a second way to increase your faith: *But be doers of the word, and not hearers only, deceiving yourselves. For if anyone is a hearer of the word and not a doer, he is like a man observing his natural face in a mirror; for he observes himself, goes away, and immediately forgets what kind of man he was.* What I see in the mirror when I first wake up is a reflection of me. I also see that there is work to do, eg., apply a little makeup if I want to enhance my appearance. God has given us all the framework in every area of our lives. We can choose to work to do our part.

If we fail to heed what we're reading and ignore what God is telling us, then our faith grows stagnant. It took faith for us to become children of God in the first place. Therefore, to increase our faith, we need to use that "measure" of faith God gives to everyone and build on it.

3. **Test the Word** - There is a difference between "testing" God by "contesting" Him (seeing how far God's patience will go with your self-will) and "testing," or proving God's Word is true. Malachi 3:9-11 (NIV) offers one practical way God says we can prove Him faithful to His Word. This passage concerns tithing and being good stewards of the things, He has given us: "Test me in this," says the Lord Almighty, "and see if I will not throw open the floodgates of heaven and pour out so much blessing that there will not be room enough to store it." As you "test" or act on what God says and experience God's blessing, your faith grows.

The process of testing the measure of faith you have may involve trials and difficulties. How can you increase your faith in those circumstances? Consider it pure joy, my brothers and sisters, whenever you face trials of many kinds because you know that the testing of your faith produces perseverance (James 1:2-3, NIV).

Remove faith stealing words that express doubt and lack (I hope, I need, or I cannot). Learn to replace them with I expect to see, I know, I am sure, or I feel confident. Align your words with Scripture and the Law of Attraction. You must understand that a limiting belief system will hinder you from reaching the place of blessings God has already planned for you. Thought to remember: God will never ask something of you that HE didn't put into you. Trust Him, Grow and Thrive. The Bible tells us in Proverbs 3:5-6, "Trust in the LORD with all thine heart; and lean not unto thine own understanding. In all thy ways acknowledge him, and he shall direct thy paths." This is an excellent reminder that we must continuously be about putting on the mind of Christ if we are to be our best in all areas of our lives.

CHAPTER 5

*H*umanitarian *L*eadership

Helping individual leaders grow extends
your influence and impact
John Maxwell

The greatest leaders are not arrogant or feel they are above everyone else, but they exude strength and confidence. Great leaders also readily recognize contributions made toward the achievement of their goals. Leaders err when their self-confidence in their skills and abilities causes them to become self-important. Being puffed up is evidence that they are not genuinely leading Gods way. Perhaps, a contributing factor to this is because of the lavish praise and accolades they receive. Leaders can quickly become accustomed to this high praise and are lulled into a state of pride without even being aware. Yes, the well-intended praise can go to 'one's head and ruin a humble leader. We all know that it feels good to have people recognize you for your ability or contribution, but when this elevation takes you to a point where you forget that it is only by the grace of God that you can do what you do, you have gone too far. This type of elevated self-worth is not what God wants for His leaders. Followers of Christ must be cognizant at all times of the temptation to take credit for what God has done and must always remember that it is God who has blessed you with your gifts in the first place and that He is the source of your success. It is not by your power or work ethic but by the grace and favor of God. Therefore, it is incumbent upon you to remain in humility, always giving Him honor for your accomplishments.

David was a great leader, but he realized that it was because of God that he was able to achieve all that he had. He knew that God was his strength and recognized that the favor of God predicated all success. His confidence was placed in God and not on his own ability. Psalm 18:29 and 32-34 King James Version (KJV) 29. For by thee I have run through a troop; and by my God have I leaped over a wall. 32. It is God that girdeth me with strength, and maketh my way perfect. 33. He maketh my feet like hinds' feet, and setteth me upon my high places. 34. He teacheth my hands to war so that a bow of steel is broken by mine arms.

Although David appeared confident when he stepped onto the scene with Goliath, we do not know his inner thoughts. Perhaps, he was thinking of this comforting scripture with every step. Psalm 23:4 "Yea, though I walk through the valley of death, I will fear no evil: for thou art with me; thy rod and thy staff they comfort me." Perhaps he was thinking like C. L. Franklin, the songwriter who penned the lyrics to "I will trust in the Lord."

"I will trust in the Lord

I will trust in the Lord.

I will trust in the Lord until I die" (repeat twice)

Regardless of his thoughts, the leader within him said, "something must be done," and he was willing to take the lead. A true leader can act even in the face of immediate danger.

Stephen Covey, American educator, author, businessman, and keynote speaker, reminds us that successful people can appear to be in control and at ease. These leaders may be contending with issues in both the professional arena as well as on the home front. However, they operate in such a manner that does not reveal their inner struggles. On the professional level, they seem in control because they have learned various techniques which help them appear cool, calm, and collected. For example, when giving a presentation or speaking, perhaps they have mastered using some of the following strategies:

1. <u>Stay hydrated</u>. This may sound simple, but I have experienced the dry cotton mouth personally, and it is no joke. It was a struggle to speak, and every word seemed to get harder and harder to force words out of a mouth as if being stuck with glue. I have also witnessed a 'speaker's dry mouth form white foam balls, which became a horrible distraction, making it almost unbearable to watch.

2. <u>Exercise to calm nerves.</u> According to research at the Mayo Clinic, exercising before an event releases endorphin, which makes you feel better. Also, pleasant social interactions have been known to help reduce anxiety adding to the calming effect.

3. <u>Visualize the desired outcomes.</u> If you are out of sight, you may look a picture that makes you happy, visualize yourself being successful, take deep breaths, or put a big smile on your face. Some even recommend assuming a power pose. Yes, the superwoman or superman pose, hands on hips and position your feet approximately two feet apart. Learn what works for you.

4. <u>Pause.</u> If you suddenly find yourself overwhelmed during a presentation, pause. Instead of fumbling and pushing through at the risk of sounding incoherent, stop and pause a few seconds. It may seem like an eternity to you, but the audience will not think a long pause is unusual. Use this time to gather your thoughts, regain your composure, return to a calm state, and begin again.

5. <u>Embrace your nervous energy.</u> Even the most experienced speakers and leaders say that they still feel some nervousness. That alone means that nervousness is not a deal-breaker. It is what you do with it that nervous energy that matters. Dr. Mike C., a fellow toastmaster, a retired high-ranking military officer, once told me that every speaker gets butterflies. He said that the important thing was to get those butterflies to fly in formation. Then the audience would interpret it as a speaker with high energy and passion. I will always remember that. So, harness those butterflies and 'don't pace.

6. <u>Be prepared.</u> Prepare for it, practice it, and expect to deliver an outstanding presentation. And always, be aware of your body gestures and movements to ensure that they purposeful and not a distraction to your performance.

Leaders are not excluded from interpersonal relationships. Although they show a high level of professional achievement, they long for healthy, caring connections. Successful people know all too well that there is a cost to their success. It is rare for anyone to say that their success came overnight honestly. Most will tell you that their success was the result of years of dedication and many, many hours of laborious effort. The interminable time spent working outside of the home is a contributing factor in many failed marriages. The hours spent on building a successful business is a contributing factor to the strained relationships between 'one's spouse and children. This does not apply to every relationship, as all leaders will not succumb to the same pressures. Nevertheless, maintaining healthy relationships will take a concerted effort and is not impossible. There should be a high level of commitment on the part of leaders to retain balance. These successful, self-aware leaders strive to keep balance in their lives by taking great effort not to neglect those they love to accomplish personal and professional goals.

Many leaders are saddened as they reflect on their lives. When looking back over the years and how they ranked their priorities, they often see personal relationships losing out to business affairs. Hindsight being 20-20, they see numerous opportunities where they could have spent more time building and maintaining individual, lasting relations throughout their career. They realize that their singleness of focus on success caused them to pay a high price. One thing is for sure, time stands still for no one, and you can never recover it. The precious time lost from enjoying your children, watching them grow, and being there supporting them along the way can never be restored. Every individual must make their own choices, but when you are "Leading 'God's Way," you will know there has to be a balance of work and rest. Genesis 2:2 says, and on the seventh day, God ended his work which he had made, and He rested on the seventh day from all His work which He had made." Jim Collins, author of Good to Great, asks the question, "Do you have a "stop doing" List?" He tells us that most of us who lead have busy undisciplined lives with an ever-expanding "to do" List. But it's when you learn to "unplug all sorts of the extraneous junk" from your schedule that you can do great things.

Success is not all about the climb. When leading 'God's way, it is about listening to the voice of God and allowing Him to guide you. How do you rest and get restored from your work week? Do you make sure you schedule activities with your spouse and family? Do you look forward to planning and taking family vacations? Or do you think about work when you should be resting? Do you routinely allow work calls, texts, and emails to spill over into your family time? Do you find yourself preoccupied with it? Do you find it difficult to still your mind for rest finding your thoughts preoccupied with work? When work associated calls interrupt your family time, do you stop and say, "Let me do this now, it will be easier than doing it later." Or, are you able to say, "this is not an emergency, it can wait? 'Let's enjoy this weekend etc."

You may be the type that says, "I have to strike while the iron is hot!" If so, I am not saying that you do not have a valid point because we know that timing is critical. However, be cautious and ask God for wisdom and insight in all things. He will give you the ability to prioritize correctly and enable you to have more balance in your life and help you to focus on the most important things. You will be able to see whether you are pursuing success over family or if you are merely taking advantage of the opportunities He has prepared for you. A slower climb to success vs. a fast rise might be something to consider when trying to maintain a healthy home life while reaching your business goals. Unfortunately, some families will already be in crisis before some leaders discover that they have missed out on something more valuable than success. Be proactive and aware of changes that may be occurring in your relationships. As you read this, take an inventory of your life and be brutally honest.

Do you feel that you are living a balanced and harmonious life? You and I both know that no one lives and balanced 50/50 lifestyle every day. That is unrealistic because there will be times when situations will require much more effort and time than usual. Nonetheless, this should not be a daily occurrence. When you consistently spend more time with work than home, familial relationships begin to suffer. Knowing this, there are things you can do. Are you willing to make the needed changes?

What are some expected outcomes of your change? If you decide to do nothing, what is one possible outcome? You might say, "I got this!" I have no problems at all with the amount of time I spend on work or with my family. If 'that's you, then I say, you are fortunate one of the rare ones. You have it all in control and are already living a wonderfully harmonious life. Congratulations! You have already succeeded. If not, wait no longer. It is essential for both physical and mental good health to attempt to have a balance between work and home. This balance or the lack, thereof, will impact your overall productivity and sense of well-being. A balanced life is necessary, so families and loved ones will not suffer from a feeling of abandonment or neglect by your absence.

> Note: the absence that loved ones' feel is not only when you are physically away but also when you are with them and are distant and preoccupied with thoughts of work.

Learn to be attuned to your body and note changes that may be manifesting because of stress. Being self-aware allows you to know when you should act, lets you see when it is time to step back and adjust your hectic schedule. Ideally, you will make changes before your wok starts to spiral, and relationships begin to plummet. Or, your health begins to fail. If you don't recognize the warning signals, and family relationship disintegrates, and your body breaks down because of work-related stresses, you are not living the life God intended. It means your life is out-of-balance.

Living a harmonious life is not easy, but it can be done with some help and is necessary for preserving family bonds. Dean Smith, UNC-Chapel Hill basketball coach and winner of 879 games, possessed leadership characteristics indicative of those promoted in "Leading God's Way." He knew the job would be done better if players were not pushed contiguously in their fatigue. He recognized the importance of rest and realized that "… rested reserves play better than tired superstars. Proper rest determines job performance…" (page 88 The 12 Leadership Principles of Dean Smith). Too often, leaders will burn their midnight oil and demand that others working with them do the same, causing unnecessary burnout and fatigue for both parties. Relaxation time is crucial to individuals so that they can work towards maintaining family relationships.

Learn to set boundaries for yourself, business, and family. It will become necessary for you to take time to adjust and readjust your schedule when you see things are getting too hectic. Set aside time to reflect and see that your work aligns with your Core values and preserve the family structure. Learn to say no to good things. As a leader, your time and effort are not limitless. Saying "No" to good things is the only way you will have ample time for the best things; those things that matter most, those things that will help you fulfill your assignment. The good things may be distractions set in your way to hinder your progress.

Leaders are usually confident, self-motivated people. However, you may not see yourself the way others see you. You may see yourself as being confident and focused on the task at hand; others may see you as someone who appears aloft and unapproachable. I was recently the keynote speaker for local graduation, and they had my biography and a picture on the program. After the event, one of the ladies came up to me and said how much she enjoyed my speech. She also said, "you know, when I first saw your picture on the program, I thought you were unapproachable." Then she said, "I am just plain, I'm from New Jersey, but when you started speaking, I immediately connected with you." We chatted for a while, took a few pictures, and left as friends. Every time someone tells you something, it is an opportunity for you to see if there is a legitimate reason for their remarks. If nothing else, I became more aware of how images can impact the perceptions of others and how important the proper selection of a photo for various events can be.

Good leaders should always be approachable and able to develop and sustain relationships with those they supervise. When a leader has a healthy respect for relationships, they willingly invest in others. This investment into the development of others fosters genuine loyalty and goodwill. It creates an environment conducive for mutual respect, which further ensures the leader's continuing ability to influence. Mutual respect is a foundation of strong teams.

Leaders who have established a high-performance standard and have built a loyal team are guaranteed that the continuation of their work will be at an adequate level even when the leader is not present. There are some teams, however, that outwardly celebrate the absence of their leader. What does this say? They view it as a time to take an extended break, slack off from their regular job duties or worse yet, stop working altogether when they are not being monitored. Of course, this is an extreme example. Nonetheless, there is often a marked difference in productivity when leaders are absent for short periods, when, in fact, there should be no significant performance decrease in the daily operations at all.

"Trust in the Lord with all thine Heart and LEAN not upon thine own understanding; In all thy ways acknowledge Him, and He will direct thy paths.

CHAPTER 6

*C*ultivating *L*eaders
*T*hrough *C*oaching

"Leadership is the ability to get extraordinary
achievements from ordinary people."
Brian Tracey

As a leader, you will be recognized by what you do but also by the
accomplishments of your Team. If you are to achieve your goals
successfully, it will take a Team. Have you heard the John Maxwell
statement, "teamwork makes the dream work?" Well, it's true. The Team
must work with you. How to you get that to happen, it is made possible
through clear communication, detailed vision casting, the establishment
of goals, and strategic plans that can be executed. In addition to genuine,
respectful relationships.

Coaching is a way of moving people forward to the desired place. It
occurs through meaningful engagement, the building of rapport, and
mutual trust. This establishment of trust enables them to safely review past
actions and outcomes and is conducive to productive insight. Conversations
between the leader and others take the form of reflective discussions that
may cause a shift in perspectives— thus clarifying and creating goal-
oriented action steps. Leaders know that these coaching strategies will
enable others to rise to higher levels of performance. According to Gary
Collins, author of Christian Coaching, "coaching is a discipline of helping

people grow without telling them how to do it." Think of the increasing confidence a person will gain when they experience solving matters themselves. Many times, coaching techniques are used to help others turn their potential into reality, and you are not even thinking of it as coaching. It may come naturally, as the right way to do.

Mature leaders understand that every person differs in ability and motivation and that different strategies are required to move everyone towards excellence. They know that if they are willing to differentiate their methods to motivate and aspire, forward movement will occur. Have you ever heard that "Leading is not leading unless you are out in front" or that, "Leading from behind is called pushing?" A coaching leader will assume both roles. There will be times when they are clearly in front, demonstrating and modeling the task. There will be times when they are behind, inspiring, prompting, and supporting. Also, more often than not, they will be alongside asking those essential questions that will prompt critical thinking. It is in the best interest of all when the leader knows from what position he or she is leading, and which place is best for the group.

Kouzes and Posner are respected authorities on leadership, and their work is a reliable source for leaders in every discipline. They created a chart called The Ten Commitments of Leadership, which lists commitments that leaders should incorporate to ensure success. I don't think they will mind me taking a little liberty by calling their Ten Commitments the Ten Commandments of Leadership. The key elements found on their chart has been repeated in this book. Successful leaders must be self-aware, know their CORE values, and be willing to set an example before others. They must be vision casters and possess the ability to enlist others to service. Successful leaders will always learn from mistakes and understand the value of establishing trust and sharing power and are adept at building community. Having a strong sense of community improves communication, a sense of belonging, and enhances productivity.

There are many different leaders. Some are more managerial in nature and rarely challenges an established process. Others are change-agents and will courageously step out of the box with an innovative idea or to challenge the **status quo**. There are situations where both of these leaders can be more suited for a specific situation and time. This has me thinking of another one of my professors who said, laws were laws until they were challenged. In other words, laws are the laws because no one had challenged them and caused them to be and rewritten. Another professor said, the best candidate for the job not necessarily the most qualified, it happens to be the one the selections committee thinks is best. That was his way of saying, when you don't get the job offer, it is because they thought someone else was better, not because that person was. Don't take it personally; keep moving.

Leaders have and should use their ability to affect positive change, innovate, and improve the existing status quo. Leaders who possess a growth mindset, courageously experiment, and boldly take risks to make things better. They understand that an attempt that fails is not the end. It is merely another opportunity to revisit, revise, and grow from past mistakes. Mature leaders who challenge current processes are not attempting to do things differently just for the sake of doing it differently nor are they taking a stance to be a nonconformist who may protest all popular ideas and practices. Good leaders will go against the status quo, standard protocol, policy, etc. when seeking a means to make things better. Because this, sometimes leaders will not be seen in a positive light, maybe talked about and may feel ostracized by others.

All leader practice the inspiring a shared vision. Anyone expecting to lead others must be convinced of their mission and possess the ability to communicate it in such a way that it uplifts, inspires, and motivates others to align with their cause. This ability to organically enlist others to join your cause happens when you can appeal to their CORE values and interests. You will want to make a connection to their hopes and dreams while being authentic and genuine

Leaders practice enabling others. One of the critical elements of doing this is developing trust with your Team. When those that follow you can depend on you and your track record, they will be more willing to support you in new endeavors. Good leaders will share their authority confidently, delegate power to those they have confidence in and who they have trained or are mentoring. Fourth, a leader should be competent enough in their area to Model the Way. Leaders should be daily demonstrating the behaviors they expect from others. They should be an example or a role model for onlookers. Finally, the fifth practice is one that makes my heart sing. A great leader will share praise with those who helped make it happen. They will regularly recognize the contributions of others, both large and small, and eagerly celebrate the Team's accomplishments. This fosters confidence among all team members and serves to encourage them further to do more, work harder, and creates a greater feeling of unity among members.

However, some leaders desire all the praise for themselves. They are often offended if compliments are given to their followers without also acknowledging them. The Bible tells us to "Do unto others as you would have others do unto you."

If you ever watch sports, when there is a big win, the coach makes sure his Team gets the credit.

A coach's role is one of support on deepening one's awareness of issues and to enhance goal setting abilities. To facilitate the coaching process, coaches may use the **GROW Model** and ask the coachee these questions.

G - **Goals:** what are the important goals/outcomes of the coaching conversation? What things does the person being coached want to explore? What are the short- term goals? Long-term?

R - **Reality:** What is the status of the situation, what is happening right now? How much time are you willing to spend on the task? What support do you need?

O - **Options:** What are the available options? What are the costs associated with the goal? What are the benefits? What can be done to accomplish the desired goals? What strategic steps are needed to move from A- B.

W - **Wrap it up:** How will you be accountable for implementing the strategies? Identify barriers? What will you do to overcome them? How will you measure success? What steps will you take to reach you goal? When will it get done? What are your benchmark dates? Who will be your accountability partner? When will you start? On a scale of 1-10, how certain are you that you will follow the planed action steps? If the number is less than 10, ask, What will make it a 10? How will you celebrate your achievement?

Companies have found that group coaching has a significant impact as it shifts from individual performance to team performance. In "From One To Many" Phil Sandahl says, "Collaborative work teams can accomplish results that individual, acting alone, s imply can't. The future source for productivity improvement is with the team."

CHAPTER 7

Leadership Transcends Titles

"If your actions create a legacy that inspires others
to dream more, learn more, do more and become
more, then, you are an excellent leader."
Dolly Parton

Effective leaders must think with the end in mind. Why is that important? Leaders must first have a good vision of what they want, how it is supposed to look, feel, and what it will take to accomplish it. When they know these things within themselves, it is easier for them to share their vision with others. You know how it is when someone is trying to explain something to you, and they don't fully understand it themselves. You can become frustrated, lose interest, or simply disconnect. Be aware that people are different, and their perspectives and their thought processes are not always going to be like yours. Therefore, at these times, there is not an immediate meeting of the minds.

Over the years, there has been much research on the brain, and researchers have come up with a term called the brain dominance theory. Each side of the brain specializes in different processes. Studies found that the left side is time-bound with sequential thinking and specializes logic/ analysis and verbal information, whereas the right side is more intuitive, creative, and is more holistic in thought. In his book, "7 Principles of Highly Effective People," Steven Covey says that people tend to stay in their comfort zone by operating from their dominant hemisphere. He also notes that it would be idyllic for us to cultivate both hemispheres so that we can easily crossover between left and right sides. This would allow each issue to be resolved by the hemisphere inclined to perform optimally using its natural problem-solving propensities.

Steven Covey also talks about the "character ethic," which he believes is the foundation of success. He expounds upon the importance of character, integrity, and temperance, as well as the importance of having humility, fidelity, modesty, simplicity, patience, and courage. When I first saw his list of important characteristics, I thought how closely these characteristics paralleled the fruit of the Spirit. He states that these characteristics and the golden rule, doing unto others as you would have them do unto you, have been found consistently in ancient writings about success. It is clear to see the importance of having good character in every area of your life. When you successfully integrate the basic principles of the character ethic in your life, you will not only be successful but will be living in alignment with the WORD of God. Since God's goal for all His children is for us to be like Jesus (Romans 8:29), the Holy Spirit constantly works to rid our lives of the "acts of the sinful nature" (Gal 5:19) and displays His fruit instead. Therefore, the presence of the "fruit of the Spirit" is evidence that our character is becoming more like Christ's. The Fruit of the Holy Spirit is a recognized biblical term that emphasizes nine attributes or characteristics of people living in alignment with the Holy Spirit as recorded in Galatians; love, joy, peace, patience, kindness, goodness, faithfulness, gentleness, and self-control.

Leadership models and styles continue to change over time, and there has been a noticeable shift. Personality and power are often seen overshadowing the character ethic. Leaders have become very cunning and skillful masters of techniques that will elevate them in the eyes of others. Some are even trained in human psychology and know the impact body movement, gestures, and vocal nuances have and how they can be used as a means to influence others. There is a narrow line between motivating and aspiring versus using your influence to become a master manipulator.

Never intentionally be deceptive when trying to get people on your side. You know what I mean, saying what you know they want to hear when you know you will do it. Or, when you know that what you are saying is not true, but you still say it to garner their support. Yes, there are leadership strategies to help you influence, but you should always be sincere. Failing to do so reduces your credibility and your integrity, quotient drops. You may initially reach your goal, but in the long run, you will have damaged your credibility. Do you want to be thought of as a manipulator, or someone to be distrusted; one who will say anything to close a deal or get the job done? Your goal is always to be authentic and genuine to your core values. Operating in this manner keeps you closer to leading God's Way.

Leaders have two views, the way things are, and the ways things should be. So, no matter where you look, you will never find a leader who thinks exactly like another. They may agree on many issues, and their methodology may be similar in many ways, but they will never do precisely the same. Why? Each person's attitude and behaviors in life are based on their perceptions, and our perceptions significantly influence how we think. How we think dramatically affects how we behave. How are you thinking? Proverbs 23:7, tells us that "as a man thinketh in heart, so is he."

When we are leading God's way, leaders will not place undue or unrealistic burdens on the backs of those they lead. They will not expect their followers to shoulder what they are unwilling to bear themselves. Good leaders will not hesitate to assist their team to ensure that their goals are accomplished. This brings to mind my first experience straight out of college when I was working in the finance office of our local school district. I was the new bookkeeper, entering into a position which had been vacant for some time. Stepping into this accounts payable job would have been daunting had it not been for the fantastic finance officer, Betty J. N., who knew the massive amount of work that had to be done to make the accounts current. I will never forget how she assessed the enormity of the task, rolled up her sleeves, and modeled real leadership. Together we collected the numerous invoices, statements and other relevant information that had been piled up over time and sorted through them. Yes, believe it or not, we got down on the floor in our professional attire to delve through the heaping pile of work because the desk space was insufficient to accommodate the massive number of documents we were handling.

Almost immediately, something that was once overwhelming became manageable because of a systematic approach of organizing the chaos. Great leaders possess the ability to access the need and come up with appropriate solutions quickly. They are flexible enough to demonstrate behaviors that will result in a favorable outcome. I learned the most valuable lesson in leadership that day. Never be above what needs to be done. Those that you lead will respect you more, and you will gain their loyalty.

Great leaders must be open to refining their leadership skills. No matter what type of position you hold, leaders should commit to being lifelong learners. Our world is continually changing, and technological innovations affect all areas of our lives. If leaders fail to embrace continued growth, they risk losing relevance. A leader who is no longer able or willing to keep up with current trends in their area most often are left behind, replaced, or the organization slowly perishes. Thus, leaders learn the benefits of keeping it positive and keeping it moving. This is one area of growth that is not only useful to the leader but will significantly impact the organization. A leader with the ability to be a positive thinker brings added value where ever they are. It is true that our minds naturally fall to negative thoughts, but they can be trained to focus on the positive. 5" Positive thinking and expression help to develop compassion for oneself and for others, which also causes one to view the world through a more compassionate lens."

Positive thinking is more than just telling yourself that everything is all right, and things will work out in your favor. Thinking positively is the ability to keep your cool in an adverse situation and shows maturity. At times, this can take everything you have to do it, but it can be done. Positive thinking demonstrates the soundness of mind that helps others calmly deal with life's situations. A positive thinker can affect change in a toxic environment. Current research shows a direct correlation to anxiety and depression linked to negative thoughts. On the other hand, positive thoughts have been found to help alleviate negative emotions and attitudes. How can we retrain our brains to be more positive? We can use mantras, something as simple as "I walk in peace." I must confess that there were times in my career that I used that very mantra. While walking through the halls, my steps were a rhythmic cadence to "I Walk In PEACE." It works using positive affirmations is another method of increasing your positivity. Continuous positive thinking eventually helps create new neural pathways in the brain, causing positive thinking to become automatic. Why should leaders be positive thinkers? Leaders can set the tone and atmosphere for your building or organization. As a leader, your ability to set the tone for your organization is critical. Everyone will be watching to see how you do; therefore, you need to make your first steps count. Start by establishing your presence: be visible setting examples, showing your priorities, and modeling expectations. These simple activities will quickly let your team know what kind of leader you are and what you expect them. Once you have established the mood, your attitude becomes contagious.

There will undoubtedly be days when you are not at the top of your game. Regardless of how you feel, your effort in showing your team an upbeat and optimistic leader will pay off. When you are consistent in your mood, your team will take their cues from you, many will mirror your attitude. Conversely, if your attitude is unpleasant, it can negatively impact the working environment.

The days of sitting behind a desk barking out orders are over. In the June 2019 Toastmasters Magazine article, "**Hubris**: Leadership's Fatal Flaw?" Jane Seago says, "hubristic leaders are convinced of their omniscience, they see no reason to talk to and learn from their employees, who can offer useful perspectives." Leaders must be willing to interact with people. Learn to be cordial and don't let others observe you speaking to some and ignoring others. Show the same courtesy to everyone encounter. It doesn't cost you anything to show interest in others, and it may earn you big rewards. Depending on your personality, it may be difficult for you not to monopolize conversations. Nonetheless, allow team members to talk about things of interest to them. Listening shows you value their thoughts, and they will become comfortable sharing openly with you.

Trust me; there will be times when you will need to know what they or other team members may be thinking. You will want to keep this communication link open.

Good leaders are emotionally mature. This maturity makes it easier to assume blame when challenges arise. A lack of self-confidence and negative thinking patterns will cause unmatured leaders to quickly cast blame. While a confident leader will more readily assume responsibility for personal feelings, thus creating a better working environment. Consider these suggestions for increasing your positive thinking:

➢ Write down positive comments in a journal.

➢ Learn to celebrate things that were enjoyable or small achievements on that day.

➢ Participate in pleasant things (they can be as simple as chatting with an old friend, listening to music or whatever brings you joy and happiness).

➢ Display photos, or any evidence of success as a visual reminder.

➢ Think about a time or place when you were pleased.

The bible supports the importance of this thinking positively. Philippians 4:8 says, "Finally brethren, whatsoever things are true, whatsoever things are honest, whatsoever things are just, whatsoever things are pure, whatsoever things are of good report if there be any virtue and if there be any praise, think on these things…"

Myles Munroe once said, "good leaders employ, great leaders, deploy." To employ, simply stated, means that you have the authority to provide work for others and pay them for it. This leader can hire and recruit others for paid services. Great Leaders Deploy. When I heard this, I thought of our military troops. They are in service awaiting the commands of their superior officers. When they get their orders, they have already been trained and equipped for the jobs they are called to do. The troops then move into position for military action. These men and women are deployed to strategic locations and are expected to be successful in their respective position/place.

5 Levels of Leadership, John Maxwell

Level 1 is the lowest level of leadership. At this level, people follow you because your title or position requires them to. You have employees assigned to you. They know that to get paid they must do what you say. This level only fosters compliance. Those following you at this level will often give you their minimum effort. Yes, there are some people employed whose ideas of working is to do enough so as not to get fired. These are the people who will quickly say, "this" "that" is not my job and will quickly pass you along. Now, don't misunderstand. I appreciate adherence to established protocol but there are some who make no effort to help others navigate through the protocol or give a simple answer when needed. These are the ones who are prepared to exit the building minutes before it's time to go.

Level 2 leadership is when you are building relationships, and by virtue of your connection with the people, they, in turn, permit you to lead them. Leaders at this level are not satisfied being secluded in their office. They are the ones out among the people, listening to their concerns and their ideas. These leaders are observant, looking for new ideas that can make things better for those that are in the organization. The show an attitude of servanthood, asking themselves what I can do to make things go better. Whatever the office or title, a good leader, is in there working, developing and growing. Over time, they will outgrow their position and move to the next level of leadership.

Level 3 leaders are highly productive; they are producers. They model the way and show others how. I need to pause a moment to make sure you understand these leaders are not manipulative. They are passionate about what they believe and the value that it will bring to you, so they present in a way that is readily accepted. Level 3 leaders produce momentum.

Level 4 people develop a passion or commitment to growing other people, and they want to increase the capacity of those around them. They know that recruitment is a crucial element. They see the qualities in others and are eager to get that person into the right position. They understand that skill and correct positioning is essential to success. You can be highly skilled but in the wrong place and fail. Example: Excellent reference and very knowledgeable Nurse but didn't love children. That is when you have to have critical conversations with people that will move them forward or out. I particularly like that Level 4 leaders are concerned about the development of others. They consistently help develop and increase the capacity of others. These leaders are fully committed to equipping, enriching and stimulating others to be better. They know the importance of:

1. Recruitment-getting the right people.
2. Position-getting people in the organization in the right place.
3. Equipping others with the tools and information needed to do their jobs efficiently.

Level 4 leaders' behavior says: I can confidently do it, watch me.

I can do it with you while you are learning how.

You will be equipped to do it independently.

I will be here to watch and support you as you do it.

Now, get someone else to do it.

Level 5, according to Maxwell, this is the pinnacle. Rarely does a leader reach this level. By the time a leader has reached this level, they have not only mastered the lower four levels, but they now possess a high degree of skill. Level five leaders are skilled at developing other leaders. By doing so well, they have created a legacy within the organization. These leaders elevate the entire organization by creating an environment that is beneficial to everyone and display gratitude and humility. Their sphere of influence extends far beyond their organization.

Jim Collins, author of Good to Great, also talks of these level 5 leaders. He says, "Whereas the good to great companies had Level 5 leaders who built an enduring culture of discipline, the unsubstantiated comparisons had Level 4 leaders who personally disciplined the organization through sheer force."

The first part of Matthew 5:16 says, "Let Your light so shines before men that they may see your good works." Dr. Myles Munroe was one of my favorite speakers on leadership. I still enjoy reading and listening to his thoughts on or about leadership. His philosophy on developing a successor agreed with the management guru, Peter Drucker, who stated, "There is no success without a successor." That is a powerful statement. A leader's lasting achievement is a reality only if it continues after they are gone.

You must possess the power of influence and get people to thrive through inspiration and not manipulation. Leaders should have the desire and the capacity to deploy. Good leaders employ, great leaders deploy. Leaders push people to become who they are. In your words, what are the traits of a good leader?

LEADING GOD'S WAY

Foundational traits of a leader

First, you must discover your purpose. Your purpose is your "why!" Some people seem to have been born knowing what they wanted to do but a greater number of us find it along the way. There are some who are well into adulthood are still asking the question, "what is my purpose?" Discovering your life's purpose is easier from some than others so don't be discouraged. Keep seeking through prayer for your answer.

God has equipped you for your assignment, that special something that you were created to do? Slow down and think about what it is that you are passionate about, tap into that passion and be confident in it. Believe you can do that which you were purposed. You alone are responsible for defining your purpose. People are entitled to their views and always have them, but you do not have to accept them as yours. Don't allow the thoughts and opinions of others to derail or minimize what you know to be your purpose. Purpose is not something that you can just think your way into, it comes with a feeling. You feel compelled to do, act your way, and work your way into it. It often evolves out of your *doing*. What is it that you are doing most? My question to you is, are you operating from your head, or, your heart? When asked this question, some folk may give a blank stare. What do you mean "operating from my head or heart?" Operating from your head results in you making decisions based on these factors: the status quo, ordinary and accepted practices, practicality, and perhaps choosing a more cost effective or less laborious method. Although operating from the head may be practical, it seldom provokes you to become the best person you can be. God speaks to the heart, learn to listen. Your heart is the best tool to access your real purpose and propel you forward, accomplishing great things. What are you doing that makes your heart sing? The best leaders are those who can connect to their passion. When you are passionate, it gives you the confidence to assume risk. For these leaders, their work is a labor of love. How passionate are you about your assignment? I know we must have money to live, but if money wasn't an issue, would you still want to do what you are doing?

The reality of it is that discovering your purpose happens when you understand the importance of being authentically YOU and living in alignment with whom God created you to become. It takes time for reflection and introspection. Our purpose is as unique as our journey. It is important to know that along the way, people will offer you their opinions, ideas, and suggestions for your use. (Might I add they may also be very forceful in trying to convince you that their views are the correct one's for you). However, only you can define your unique purpose. You alone, with prayer and the right tools, can determine this. Caution: Do not undervalue your God-given ability or measure yourself against another person. God determines how far you will go. Your job is to do your due diligence and work as unto the Lord.

We all have heard that everything happens for a reason. What exactly does this term mean? Do we believe it, or is it something that we say to feel better when things go wrong in life? The bottom line is that we can learn from every situation we face in our lives, good or bad. We have the choice to make a conscious decision to benefit and grow or become bitter. In negative situations I purposely choose to FOCUS (Fearlessly Optimize Challenges Until Success). With that attitude, sometimes the most difficult challenges are turned into the biggest blessings. When you believe things will get better, you will not fall into despair. During tough situations, learn to step back, remove the emotion that is sometimes attached to the event or situation, and begin to look at it through God's perspective. That is when you will find it easier to go through, relying on Romans 8:28.

Living authentically should be easy but that is not always so. Why? Because we are products of our environment. There are numerous factors affecting our behaviors. Sometimes because of our natural skill in an area, people will want us to do this or that. Or, because of our height they may assume we love sports and should be a competitive athlete. We are also heavily influenced by our families and society. We may tend to follow paths that seem natural because of this or that. How many people make decisions on their careers, hobbies, and relationships, based on familial expectations or social conditioning simply because "we should" rather than because it feels true to what our hearts say. Choices made because of these factors often leave us unsatisfied and less successful. It takes effort to be true to yourself, but it is well worth your effort. Be intentional in your effort to live a life on purpose, means using your God given talents, your natural interests, and live in alignment with who God has created you to be. Learn to be Unapologetically You and uncover your true purpose. Passion + Daily Action = Purposeful Life. Vision comes once you are convinced about your purpose. You will begin to see a preferred future. Habakkuk 2:2-3 "And the Lord answered me: 'Write the vision; make it plain on tablets, so he may run who reads it. For still the vision awaits its appointed time; it hastens to the end—it will not lie. If it seems slow, wait for it; it will surely come; it will not delay.'" Vision is to see a future as it should be and not as it is. There is only one difference between a manager and a leader. A manager sees things as they are, but a leader sees things as they should be. A leader is someone who sees a better future and is willing to pay the price to bring that future to the present.

Once you discover your purpose and have a vision, you must become passionate about it. Your passion will propel you forward through both good days and bad. Passion will tell you, "You can," when everything around you says, "No, you can't." And finally, you have the ability to influence others to inspire. You have become a motivator and inspire people to aspire. People see the evidence of your leadership.

According to Dr. Myles Munroe, there's a difference between vision and ambition. Ambition is when you are looking for something to benefit you. Whereas, a vision benefits not only you and your generation, but generations to come. A vision is linked to a greater good. Is there a link between leadership and legacy? Leadership can impact us now, but a legacy continues to impact others even after we are gone. For this reason, it is extremely important for leaders to be involved in mentorship. Mentorship is a critical element in leadership. When a leader has a vision that is true and authentic, it will always be bigger than the visionary. That's why leaders must identify people that connect with their vision and mentor them to take the helm after the leader's work career or life has ended. Yes, I believe that one of the greatest acts of leadership is mentorship. Leaders that take the time to impart knowledge, wisdom, and skills, to help someone else is, according to John Maxwell, a Level 4 leader. A Level 4 leader will invest their time, energy, money, and thinking, into growing others as leaders. Good leaders will seek to find the potential in every person and attempt to gauge his or her potential to grow. Good leaders will be open and not be affected by the individual's title, position, age, or experience. This practice of developing people is often a catalyst for bringing out the best in the team.

A vision is never given to a group of people but to one person at a time. The task of a true leader is not just to acquire the vision, but also to define and refine the vision, to write it down and to transfer it to people who will run with it—this is when legacy takes effect, when the baton is successfully passed. This requires vision casting:

➢ Crisis-communicate an urgent need that connects with an emotional level. Define the problem or crisis. Why do they need to act now? Why is it unacceptable to do nothing?

➢ Compelling Messages-drives the audience to action. Communicate a clear call to action. What be done? What is the solution?

➢ Clarity-Clarify the steps you're asking people to take. Make them simple, clear, and logical. Then, tell them how they are supposed to respond?

➢ Creativity-What makes your vision different than what they have already heard. How can you say it in a new way?

Why is legacy so important? Legacy is important because the need to intentionally prepare for someone to take your place is critical when the vision is to be sustained. I love this Myles Munroe quote, "Success without a successor is failure." This quote is from one of 'Dr. Monroe's final interviews with lancet. There is no legacy without mentorship! If you fail to prepare for your legacy, the chances of your vision dying with you is great. This is a stark reminder that the quality of your leadership is not only determined while you are still around. Dr. Myles Munroe said, "when I'm gone that's when you will see if I managed to transfer my vision, my passion, and my conviction to the next generation." How are you impacting the world? Once you know who you are, understand the assignment, get busy doing what you were created to do, then, mentor others. YES, pass it on.

CHAPTER 8

The Straight Path to Leadership

"Every stumble is not a fall, and every fall is not a failure."
Oprah Winfrey

When we choose to Lead God's Way, you will use God's methods to get his people where He wants them in reliance on his power." Why decide to lead Gods way when there are so many leadership styles that work well. As believers of Christ, I believe that we should desire to model our behavior after Him. As spiritual leaders, we want to glorify Him through our work. Also, when our goal is to lead like Christ, we are more interested in transformation rather than dictating and directing people. We aim to develop people, so their desire becomes getting to where God wants them to be. We all are leaders in some degree and have responsibility for leadership in some relationships.

Spirit-filled leaders, glorify God, have confidence in Him and pray for His guidance, always acknowledging that it is He who sustains them in all things. What do Spirit-filled leaders do?

1. **Glorify God and desire that others come to glorify Him.** According to Matthew 5:14–16, one-way others can see God in you is by your behavior. When others see you treating people who like or who dislike you with the same kindness and compassion, they will see you modeling the love of God. Yesss, "you are the

light of the world." I have always said that believers of Christ should not have to walk into the workplace saying, "Praise the Lord Everybody!" for others to know that they are Christians. It is a committed lifestyle, and daily conversations and behaviors should exemplify that fact.

2. **Possess faith and confidence.** When we have faith in the goodness of God, we trust that things will work themselves out in love. Romans 8:28. When we believe God, it strengthens us for the work. Regardless of the situation, we can confidently cast our cares on Him. We are confident in the outcome and are not looking for scapegoats to take the blame for our failures nor are we busily trying to manipulate the circumstances to make ourselves look better. When our hope is strong, we are free from paralyzing fears that prohibits the free exercise of love. Therefore, a spiritual leader must be a person who has strong faith and in the sovereign goodness of God and confidence everything will work out as it is intended. Otherwise, he may inevitably fall into the trap of exploiting others and manipulating circumstances.

3. **Pray for Guidance.** Leaders seek God's guidance for decision-making ability, clarity of situation, and for help and wisdom to lead.

4. **Acknowledge Him.** When you acknowledge your need for God, you will not fail in your prayer and meditation. You will go before Him humbly knowing that it is because of Him that you can achieve. You understand that to lead effectively, you must continually seek to know Him through fasting, the study of the WORD, and prayer.

LEADING GOD'S WAY

When leading God's way, you may feel:

1. Restlessness

Leaders that are being guided by God are often dissatisfied with the **status quo**. They want to make things better, to grow and reach out to others. These leaders realize that God expects them to promote actions that are aligned with His Word. These leaders are optimistic but still prepare for an uphill climb, knowing that God is always present.

2. Intensity/Or urgency for completion

Godly leaders are task focused and have an excellent work ethic. They are driven to do it right. Ecclesiastes 9:10, "Whatever your hand finds to do, do it with all your might." Often these leaders must pull away from a variety of social distractions. This time of solitude provides them with the opportunity to spend more time with God.

3. Self-Control

Discipline and self-control enable leaders to stay the course until the job is done. This determination means that they will not allow the feelings of emotions to deter their progress or alter their course. According to Galatians 5:23, discipline is seen as self-control, a fruit of the Spirit.

4. Mental Strength

Any leader who constantly craves affirmation from others will certainly be an ineffective leader. The very nature of leadership says you must be strong enough to stand with or without support. And if you thrive on the approval of others, your decisions will be impacted by what will garner you the most approval. When this happens, you are no longer leading but you are being led by others. My advice to you is to be able to pull from your inner strength when your supporters are few. And when you make a bad decision, acknowledge it, learn from it and move on. The sooner you get over it, the better off you will be. The Bible tells us in in 2 Corinthians 4:8,9, "We are afflicted in every way, but not crushed; perplexed, but not driven to despair; persecuted, but not forsaken; struck down, but not destroyed." When you feel burdened by criticism pray, keep your chin up and don't lose hope. This too shall pass. The reality of it is that no leader is excluded from trying times and no significant spiritual leader comes from people who are always seeking affirmation.

5. Enthusiasm

As I was doing my research for this book, I came across an article by John Piper, "The Marks of a Spiritual Leader," which says, "lazy people cannot be leaders. Spiritual leaders redeem or [make] the best use of the time," (Ephesians 5:16). I thought about that for a while then began to think about the spiritual leaders that I know and admire. I found that I had to agree with him. Good leaders will find that there is always a lot going on, and the pressures of deadlines and obligations can become overwhelming. But, it is during this time that they need to be reminded of something they already know. Leaders must practice self-care and make it an intentional part of their schedule. Learn to take care of yourself; your body needs both mental and physical rest. It will prove beneficial in the workplace and at home. Exhausted people do not perform at their optimum capacity.

6. Clarity and Good Judgment

A good leader can look at situations, be self-aware enough to recognize personal biases they have that might cause them to make irrational decisions.

> Note: *Acknowledge your bias.* Our brains are wired to look for patterns and causes a subconscious influence on our actions. Work to change your conditioning. **Challenge your negative bias. Learn to be empathetic and be open to dialogue.**

They are also able to distinguish between personal and professional opinions when making decisions. Critical thinking skills are a necessity and is considered a fundamental tool. In addition, leaders who know the power of prayer know that decisions are not made thoughtlessly. God should be sought to provide insight and wisdom.

In our society, we often sum up a person in just a few minutes of meeting them. These first impressions can be a real glimpse into who we are, or they can be wrong. Thank God that Jesus is concerned with us and our hearts (John 2:24–25). He urges us to be perceptive in assessing others (Matthew 7:15–20). Leaders are knowledgeable and intuitive, using their observations of others with their knowledge of the job requirements to know who is well-suited for positions.

Place your checkmark beside any of the 18 Leadership Behaviors below that you must improve upon to become a more effective leader.

Self-Assessment Check List

Leadership Behaviors		Improvement needed
1	Self-Aware	
2	Set Tone and Desired Pace	
3	Promote Unity with Organization	
4	Build Relationships of Mutual Respect	
5	Model Expected Behaviors	
6	Positive and Optimistic Attitude	
7	Provide Timely Constructive Feedback	
8	Optimize Opportunities	
9	Vision Casting	
10	Solution Oriented	
11	Informed and Open to learning	
12	Celebrate and Publish Wins	
13	Authentic and Honest	
14	Foster Team Buy-In	
15	Build Team Involvement	
16	Keep things In Proper Perspective	
17	Value Your Time and Others	
18	LISTEN! (BE Open to give and receive constructive Criticism)	

Researchers have examined leadership from a variety of perspectives over the years, finding that there is no single trait or characteristic that guarantees great leadership. You will notice that both effective and non-effective leaders can possess some similarities. Below is a model that will not guarantee success, but it will help you in getting tasks done:

Task Cycle

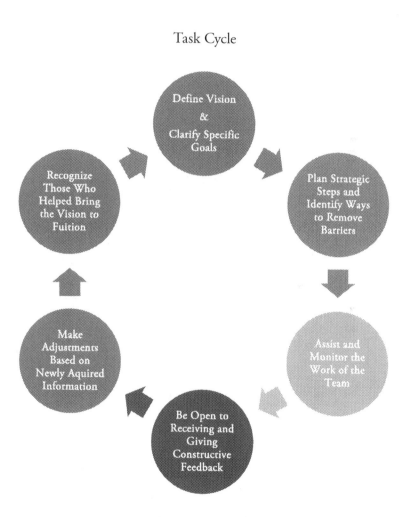

Quiz Questions

T/F		Questions
1		All Christians are good leaders.
2		Leaders are born, you either have it or you don't.
3		One of the most important characteristics of a great leader is the ability to serve.
4		Leaders are responsible for modeling, equipping, and supporting.
5		Great leaders should be reactive.
6		Your leadership is reflecting in every area of your life.
7		Leaders understand that their trust will build team confidence.
8		To lead with courage does not mean that the leader has no FEAR.
9		Good leaders know that others are to blame when they fail.
10		Benevolent leaders are always loved.

		Quiz Answer/Explanations
1	F	All Christians are not good leaders. Many must grow in humility, patience, and their desire to serve others.
2	F	Some great leaders have learned how to become leaders through their study of proven leadership principles and developing their personal leadership habits.
3	T	It is true that one of the most important characteristics of a great leader is the ability to serve.
4	T	Leaders are responsible for modeling, equipping, and supporting those they lead.
5	F	Great leaders should be proactive not reactive. Great leaders plan ahead, anticipating possible outcomes. This reduces emergencies and unexpected barriers. They build trusting relationships and take advantage of opportunities as they arise.
6	T	It is true that leadership or lack thereof is reflected in every area of your life.
7	T	Leaders understand that their trust will build team confidence. Trust comes from demonstrating trustworthiness. It is important to build an atmosphere of trust in your organization. It increases productivity and fosters a positive environment.
8	T	To lead with courage does not mean that the leader has no FEAR. This is true because in many cases, leaders may be going into uncharted waters and will not know if they will find the outcome they desire.
9	F	Good leaders know that others are to blame when they fail. This is not a true statement. Mature leaders, with a growth mindset, will accept failure as a challenge to succeed the next time.
10	F	Benevolent leaders are always loved. This is definitely false. When you are leading others, there will be times when you will not be popular. As a leader, this is not the focus of your concern. You want them to respect your character, integrity, ability and trust you have their best interest in view.

CHAPTER 9

Stepping Into Your GREATness

"People who are truly strong lift others up. People who are truly powerful bring others together."
Michelle Obama

You have chosen to read this today because you are interested in stepping up to your true greatness as a leader. This STEP Up to a new level will take effort. It will require you to change things that have become easy for you. Your desire to become a more effective leader, and one who is leading in alignment with the WORD of God, will have an impact on your life and the lives of others. You know that success is a journey of understanding who you truly are, it is about developing into the best self that you can be.

Anyone interested in leading God's way, no doubt is passionate about helping others break through their limiting belief system and interested in helping them to develop while allowing them to grow in confidence. I was once held hostage by my own limiting beliefs and struggled to first identify them. Then I began the journey to eradicate the untruths which changed my thoughts and in turn changed my behaviors. So, I understand the process and how important it is to have a leader who is committed to your growth.

If you have made it this far in the book, I thank you for partnering with me on this assignment to empower others and help move them towards their true potential while reminding them that they possess GREATness within. My goal is to help build stronger communities of self-assured, confident people (particularly women), who embrace their uniqueness and can celebrate the differences in others, thereby improving their lives and making the world a better place.

I saw this quote recently and it resonated with me, "Success is not what you get, but whom you become." Are people who amass wealth successful even though they lack character and integrity and fail to give back to their community? Helping others become successful can be a daunting goal but one we can do collectively. When we choose to live a life without limits, where all things are possible to those who believe it is in their future. We begin to move towards **self-actualization**. And when we know it can be done, we are better able to help others. As leader, you must be the first partaker, you must believe that there is hope for a good future. Jeremiah 29:11is one of my favorite passages and it reminds us that God has plans for our good future. And since we know that God is a purposeful God and that all things were constructed on purpose for a purpose, we can believe that there is nothing that He considers "just for the sake of it." Everything God puts His hands or His Words on is intentional and purposeful. Rest assured that there will be many times when His purposes aren't immediately apparent to us. That is when we must depend on our faith to carry us through.

Leaders have a tremendous amount of responsibility and often succumb to depression. You should not be surprised that one in five people today struggle with depression, which is often rooted in a state of purposelessness. Recommended treatments usually involve methods to re-establish the individual's sense of purpose: 1. they are creating a routine 2. setting goals 3. taking on responsibilities 4. doing something new, or 5. volunteering for a cause. This reinforces how our beliefs directly impact our lives and why it is essential to know and stand on the truth of God's Word. God's Word assures us that He has an excellent plan for us. Trust His Word and know that the circumstances of today will not harm you. God will use them all to prepare you for what is ahead. Enjoy where you are on the way to where you are going.

Affirmation Words are powerful, and they increase your faith. Here are a few to repeat when doubt starts to undermine your confidence: It is possible, God has great plans for me! I am anointed for this. I am God's creation; I am created for GREATness! I am His masterpiece, designed for a good purpose. He shapes my circumstances and guides my steps to fulfill His plan, and I trust Him. I am reminded not to be anxious in adverse situations, I walk in peace; I can enjoy the journey, God is in control.

Tim Ferris says that ... "you are the average of the five people that you associate with most, so do not underestimate the effects of your pessimistic, unambitious, or unorganized friends. If someone isn't making you stronger, they are making you weaker." Have you noticed that when you are walking with someone, your steps, your stride changes, until your pace become synchronized, your gait becomes matched, you begin to walk alongside? Who slows down, who speeds up? No one knows or pays attention, it just happens unconsciously.

Self-awareness is critical to your growth. It helps lets you know where you are in order to identify the steps to move you where you want to be.

Ask yourself these questions:

1. How do you want to interact with others? What brings you the greatest joy? Do this routine self-monitoring as your perspective may change over time.
2. Be Enthusiastic/Generate Energy so you can maintain focus, effort, and well-being. Your positive energy will also draw others to you. Stay Focused and stay on your game. Take time for self-care; you'll need to care for your mental health, physical stamina, and positive emotions.
3. Strive for excellence. Raise the necessity for exceptional performance. Be motivated on your way! This means actively tapping into the important reasons you desire to achieve the goal. This necessity is based on your CORE VALUES (identity, beliefs, values, or expectations for excellence) and external demands (social obligations, competition, public commitments or deadlines).
4. Increase productivity and brand awareness in your field of interest. Specifically, focus on prolific quality output and minimize distractions. Know that some seemingly good opportunities can be distractions that steal your time and attention from your primary focus and goals

5. Develop your personal field of influence with those around you. Your sphere of influence (character/integrity/community involvement) impacts how willing people will be to support your efforts and ambitions. Develop a support team, network to ensure that significant achievements are possible.

6. Demonstrate courage by boldly expressing your ideas, and bravely standing up for yourself and others, even in the face of fear, uncertainty, threats, or changing conditions. Courage is not an occasional act, but a trait of choice and will.

Growth Strategies:

1. Find a mentor, someone who will take the time to share their knowledge with you. Ask someone that you trust and possesses the ability to connect you with others who can help you fulfill your vision. When it comes to leading, you will not have all the answers, and don't expect to. Use your resources and connect with others who are knowledgeable in areas that you are not.

2. Membership in other organizations and affiliations is a means of getting your message out there. If you are a Lone Ranger, your reach will not extend very far.

3. Take time to nurture existing relationships and work towards fostering new ones. When it comes to leading you must develop some social skills. If you have a natural propensity to be an introvert, this is not a detrimental factor to your leadership. You can learn how to increase your social engagement. Introverts and Extroverts can make great leaders.

4. Develop a Positive Attitude. As the leader of your organization, your attitude has the power to change the environment. You can determine whether there will be a positive or negative change. Avoid pessimism at all cost.

Leadership is not for the faint of heart. Brad Lomenick states in H3 Leadership that "Excellence is what helps a leader and an organization move from competent to exceptional." Leaders are held accountable by others, and they must also hold themselves accountable. To forge ahead in leadership, it is to your advantage to be mature and to understand your "why." When you are committed to the "why," you are doing a thing, it strengthens your resolve in those times when you don't know "how" it can be accomplished. The ultimate responsibility of an organization's outcome will fall on the shoulder of its leaders. Don't be that person who will look for opportunities to blame others or throw them under the bus when mistakes are discovered. Like it or not, at the end of the day the responsibility lies with the leader. If the project did not meet success, what part did you play in its failure? Did you fail in some way, perhaps, by not selecting the right person to do the job? Did you provide them with all they needed (training, resources and time) to get the job done? Did you carefully monitor the process and provide adequate feedback? Were you aware of the barriers and challenges they encountered while working and did you fail to offer solutions? Did you seek experts to assist in areas where you and your team members lacked expertise? If you did all these things, there is no need to blame anyone. Only review what did not work, what went wrong, and note what went well. Is the goal still feasible? If so, rethink the process, come up with a revised plan, and try it again.

Make sure your plans consist of **SMART** GOALS. **SMART** is a mnemonic acronym, referring to the strategic steps needed for successful goal-setting. **SMART** goals will ensure that you remain focused and accountable, ultimately achieving set goals.

*S*pecific objectives are communicated to everyone involved. Communicate what it is that you want the team to accomplish. Let them know why this goal is essential. Define the roles, which are required, and at what capacity. Are there any resource limitations? What are they? How will you circumvent this shortage?

*M*easure your success in small increments so that you can celebrate your wins along the way. Carefully break down larger tasks into smaller more attainable ones that can be easily checked off. This is the place where you identify benchmarks, timelines, and what will be the evidence of completion or success?

*A*ttainable and achievable Plan of Action. This means that the desired goals can be met. Is this a realistic goal for your skill level, financial resources, etc. What are the strategic steps that need to be put into place to reach the desired goal? What are the barriers? What can be done to reduce or eliminate the barriers? Is your team able to solve any challenges or problems that would prohibit the acquisition of identified goals?

*R*esult-Focused Outcomes that are reasonable and relevant. Is it the right time to pursue this goal, does the goal align with the organization's goals? Does the amount of effort required, and resources needed make this goal prohibitive at this time, or is the goal well work all the effort and resources that will be expended?

*T*ime-Bound goals are expected to be completed within a predetermined amount of time. Carefully estimate the amount of time needed to complete each stage of the project. Routinely monitor the progress and stay in communication with all stakeholders involved.

LEADING GOD'S WAY

Do you have enough faith to believe it can be done?

Hebrews 11:1 King James Version (KJV), "Now faith is the substance of things hoped for, the evidence of things not seen." Anyone in leadership must rely on their faith. They must believe that what they are attempting to do is possible. Great leaders possess Unyielding FAITH - believe that your desired outcome is possible. If you lose faith, you lose hope and when you lose hope it is easy to stop trying. Don't give up. There is "NO" mysterious formula for Greatness. It takes hard work, time and commitment. Persistence can sometimes trump ability. Think about it, if you have the skill but are not willing to apply yourself to the extent that it takes to accomplish the task, someone with lesser ability, more tenacity and drive who will stay the course can accomplish what you fail to achieve. You must begin one step at a time. If you never start your journey, you will certainly never find your way to the end. Commit to becoming a lifelong learner. Leaders who refuse to learn will soon be left behind by those who will. Enlist others to help with your cause. When you create a strong, cohesive team it exponentially increases your efforts. Never quit (You don't have to be perfect keep trying to do your best)!

When you are passionate about what you are doing, and you want it right, it can be frustrating not to have it perfect. Remember, perfection is rare, so keep doing our best. Our best is all that is required of us!

Les Brown says once you commit you will figure it out along the way. There are some things in life that you will not know what will happen until you begin trying.

> Note: Be clear on what it is that you want to achieve. Do your due diligence, prepare, get your mind right, stretch, be willing to take the risk, commit and stay in the game.

Reminders:

1. Be self-Aware (how bad do you want to it/do you want to win?)
2. Believe that it is possible (You must identify what your "IT" is)
3. Remind yourself via positive affirmations
4. Access your FAITH

5. Be Courageous and Keep the Faith

Leading God's way is never controlling or leading others by intimidation and threats. When you lead by fear, it disempowers the ones you lead. And although this tactic may appear to work for a short while, its long-term effects can create a hostile environment. Employees controlled by fear become insecure, unmotivated and work in a survival mode. They become disinterested in the organizations' vision and look inward to their own job security. An organization with fearful people that are afraid to communicate openly and honestly, is a dysfunctional organization that does not foster creativity, innovation nor loyalty. On the other hand, when you lead with respect, you empowered others to do more. You can see the potential in others, and your desire is to help maximize their ability. You are willing to mentor, monitor, and delegate opportunities that will stretch them. Leaders that respects their team will accept suggestions, ideas, or feedback and will work together to resolve issues, thus, creating a sense of pride within the group.

It is important for every leader to know their own strengths and weaknesses. Fear is a tactic used when the leader fears their ability to get the job done any other way is slim, or there is an urgency. Often, some other insecurities may be the driving force which the leader may or may not even be aware of. You do not want to be the leader leads with fear. Fearful people usually wear an obligatory disguise made to like respect. Can you believe they would show disingenuous respect for you? Yes, remember, we said they are operating in survival mode.

Respected leaders regularly appreciate employees, regardless of their position. They know that everyone on the team has value and that it takes a team to make things work efficiently. I encourage you to be the roe model leader that desires to set a visible example of what others will aspire to become. Be the inspiration to others through your daily actions and efforts. I challenge you to be that "Wheel Turner" who will with or without a title still perform as a leader and continue to earn the respect of those around you.

CHAPTER 10

$\mathcal{B}$ecoming a $\mathcal{L}$eader

"If you want to build a ship, don't drum up the men to
gather wood, divide the work, and give orders. Instead,
teach them to yearn for the vast and endless sea."
Antoine de Saint-Exupéry

Becoming a leader is the ability to take action and apply principles that
work. A principle is a fundamental truth that serves as the foundation
for a system of belief or behavior. Regardless of who is using it the
principle, it remains the same. While studying for my masters in school
administration, one of the leaders we were required to explore was Attila
the Hun, the barbarian. Attila the Hun was one of the greatest barbarian
rulers of his time. He attacked the Roman Empire, invaded the southern
Balkan provinces and Greece, and eventually made it to Italy. He died in
453. You may be wondering, "Why in the world would this barbarian's
leadership be worthy of exploration by future school administrators?"
Particularly, why should anyone writing a book called "Leading God's
Way" include any reference of him? The truth is this, people in the world
system have tapped into proven principles because they work. Saints and
sinners alike have applied and benefited from following certain principles.
Although these principles work, the Bible clearly tells us of the outcome in
Proverbs 29:2, "When the righteous are in authority, the people rejoice: but
when the wicket beareth rule, the people mourn." This lets us know that
the unrighteous can be effective leaders, but the people will suffer. Let's
just look at excerpts from "The Leadership Secrets of Attila The Hun."

Below a few leadership strategies that Attila is said to have shared with his chieftains to help them rule more effectively:

Attila's Leadership Secrets	What does the Bible Say?
"Grant small rewards for light tasks. Reserve heaps…for dangerous, gallant, substantial effort …" Page 78	**Romans 2:6** Who will render to every man according to his deeds:
"…Share your riches with those who are loyal and stand in need." Page 78	**1 Timothy 5:18** Thou shalt not muzzle the ox that treadeth out the corn. And, The labourer *is* worthy of his reward.
"Be generous with small tokens of appreciation-they will multiply in returned loyalty and service." Page 79	⁸But if any provide not for his own, and specially for those of his own house, he hath denied the faith, and is worse than an infidel.
"Sincere concern for and purposeful mingling with your Huns will raise their spirits and encourage greater valor." Page 78	Philippians 2:4 Everyone should look out not only for his own interests, but also for the interests of others.
	1 Thessalonians 5:11T therefore encourage one another and build each other up as you are already doing. –
"In negotiation you must take well-studied risks." Page 84	Luke 14:31-32 Or what king, going out to encounter another king in war, will not sit down first and deliberate whether he is able with ten thousand to meet him who comes against him with twenty thousand? And if not, while the other is yet a great way off, he sends a delegation and asks for terms of peace.
"Momentary loss of self-worth…are normal emotions…but do not dwell too long on your bad moments." Page 88 "Huns should be taught to focus on opportunities rather than on problems." Page 108	Philippians 4:8 "Finally, brethren, whatsoever things are true, whatsoever things *are* honest, whatsoever things *are* just, whatsoever things *are* pure, whatsoever things *are* lovely, whatsoever things *are* of good report; if *there be* any virtue, and if *there be* any praise, think on these things."
"…we would accomplish more if Huns behaved as though national goals were …as personal goals." Page 106	**Ephesians 4:3** "Make every effort to keep yourselves united in the Spirit, binding yourselves together with peace."
"A Hun without purpose will not know when he has achieved it." Page 106 Chieftains should always aim high…than seeking the safe path of mediocrity." Page 106	Habakkuk 2:2 "And the Lord answered me, and said, Write the vision, and make it plain upon tables, that he may run that readeth it."
"A Hun's perception is reality for him." Page 107	Proverbs 23:7 "For as he thinketh in his heart, so is he…"

Leaders learn about other leaders. They study what works and what does not. They look at how decisions are made and catalog it for future use. It is important to knowing who you are and be accepting your characteristic for what they are. You will be able to identity some of those same characteristics in others. When you become fully self-aware you will be well on your way to becoming a good leader.

What are your personality traits and/or habits that might impede good leadership? These can change overtime, but the good news is, you change what you do and not who you are. For example, if you are an introvert but your job demands that you meet new people all the time, it doesn't change you from being an introvert. But, it does change what you do. You know you need to smile more, speak with people more often, and engage in activities more frequently, so you increase those actions. You can alter your actions to meet the need when leading.

Throughout this book, we have been talking about various strategies and about building community and managing teams — all of these things we have discussed come from getting to know people, having empathy, communicating. And no matter what your leadership style is and regardless of your personality type, these are all things you can do. Become a leader requires a mindset shift. You must believe you can and then commit to finding the methods that works best for you. Leaders are not instantly made overnight, it is a process of trial and error. The challenge yourself to become better. Be open for honest feedback on your leadership, find a mentor, someone who excels at what you want to do. And study other leaders, watch them and see what works for them. Practice looking at things from different perspectives. Work to increase your problem-solving ability. Doing these things will continue moving you forward as a leader.

What will people say about your leadership when you are gone? Will they say you:

- created excellent results and was modest about accomplishments,
- produced long-term results demonstrating calm determination and resolve,
- set high standards and empowered others for success,
- appreciated the contributions of others and readily shared credit with others.

If so, then you have demonstrated Leading God's Way.

STEPS TO SALVATION

"Through salvation our past has been forgiven, our present is given meaning, and our future is secured."
Rick Warren

This entire book has been sharing insight on ways to lead in a manner that would be approved by our model leader, Jesus. I, if you are a reader who has not made a commitment to be a follower of Christ, but you have a desire to do better and model the characteristics of Christ. Allow this book to be a new beginning for you. Not only becoming a better leader but a fresh new beginning as a Christian. Salvation was never intended to be complicated. Sins are washed away through faith in Jesus. Romans 10:9 states, "If thou shalt confess with thy mouth the Lord Jesus, and shalt believe in thine heart that God hath raised Him from the dead, thou shalt be saved." Simple enough, Acknowledge Your Sins, Confess and Believe. You can say this prayer right this moment.

Father, forgive me for my sins. I accept your Son, Jesus Christ into my life. I believe that He died on Calvary and shed His blood as the atonement for my sins. I believe that He rose from the grave that I might be saved. Fill me, O'God, with your Holy Spirit that I might live as an effective witness to others, for your Glory. Amen

That's it; God honors the sincerity of your prayers. Know that the Grace of God saves you. The choice to accept salvation is always yours. The abiding Holy Spirit will aid you along your journey. Find a church in your area if you do not have a church home. If you do attend a local church, tell your pastor of your decision to accept Christ. Use care from this moment forward and remove yourself from sinful temptations. God has forgiven you of your past sins and has given you a new life. Look into your future with high expectations of good. Connect yourself with other believers who can help strengthen you as you grow your faith. God loves you and has plans for your good future, Jerimiah 29:11. There is GREATness in you!

RESOURCES

"1 TIMOTHY 5:18 KJV For the Scripture Saith, Thou Shalt Not Muzzle the Ox That Treadeth out the Corn. And, The Labourer [Is]..." *1 TIMOTHY 5:18 KJV "For the Scripture Saith, Thou Shalt Not Muzzle the Ox That Treadeth out the Corn. And, The Labourer [Is]...",* www.kingjamesbibleonline.org/1-Timothy-5-18/.

"5 Keys To Setting The Tone As A New Leader (Mission & Vision Focused)." *LEADx,* 26 Dec. 2018, leadx.org/articles/5-keys-setting-tone-new-leader/.

"5 Proven Benefits of Positive Thinking." Lee, Faye. *HealthPrep,* 20 Feb. 2019 healthprep.co

"2017 Top Leadership Training Companies." *Training Industry,* 2 Feb. 2017, trainingindustry.com/top-training-companies/leadership/2017-top-leadership-training-companies/.

"2019 Top Leadership Training Companies." *Training Industry,* 21 Feb. 2019, trainingindustry.com/top-training-companies/leadership/2019-top-leadership-training-companies/.

Alma, Donna. "Look to the Lord Jesus Instead of That next Something New." Claresholm Local Press, Alberta Weekly Newspaper Association, 4 June 2014.

Burton, Valorie. *Successful Women Think Differently.* Harvest House Publishers, 2012.

Collins, Gary R. *Christian Coaching Helping Others Turn Potential into Reality.* The Navigators, 2014.

Collins, Jim "Good to Great" 2001 USA Harper Collins Publishers. 10 East 53rd Street. New York, NY. 10022

Covey, Stephen R. *The 7 Habits of Highly Effective People.* Simon & Schuster, 1989.

Curtin, Melanie. "In an 8-Hour Day, the Average Worker Is Productive for This Many Hours." *Inc.com*, Inc., 21 July 2016, www.inc.com/melanie-curtin/in-an-8-hour-day-the-average-worker-is-productive-for-this-many-hours.html.

DeMers, Jayson. "How to Voice Concerns Without Seeming Negative." *Inc.com*, Inc., 24 June 2015, www.inc.com/jayson-demers/how-to-voice-concerns-without-seeming-negative.html.

"From One to Many Best Practices for Team and Group Coaching." *From One to Many Best Practices for Team and Group Coaching*, by Jennifer J. Britton, Jossey-Bass, 2013, pp. 248–248.

Fox, Maren. "Transformational Leadership vs. Servant Leadership: 3 Key Differences." *Berrett-Koehler Publishers Blog*, ideas.bkconnection.com/transformational-leadership-vs.-servant-leadership-3-key-differences.

Goleman, Daniel. "What Makes a Leader" (Organizational Influence Processes, 229-241 2003 (Google Scholar)

Howard, Kathy. "What Are the Fruit of the Spirit?" *Crosswalk.com*, Salem Web Network, 26 Mar. 2018, www.crosswalk.com/faith/spiritual-life/what-are-the-fruit-of-the-spirit.html.

Jones, Laurie Beth. "Jesus, Life Coach." Thomas Nelson Publishers, 2004.

Jones, Laurie. "Have New Stories." *Jesus, Life Coach*. Thomas Nelson Publishers, 2004, pp. 261–261.

Johnson, Jill. "Build Your Confidence." *Toastmasters*, Dec. 2018. Page 27.

"Leadership Information and Leadership News." *Forbes*, Forbes Magazine, The Very First Things A New Leader Needs to Know www.forbes.com/leadership/#416158501d66. Dec. 10, 2014.

"Level 4 – People Development: Helping Individual Leaders Grow Extends Your Influence and Impact." *John Maxwell*, 19 Sept. 2011, ww.johnmaxwell.com/blog/level-4-people-development-helping-individual-leaders-grow-extends-your-inf/.

Morin, Amy. "How An Authentic 'Thank You' Can Change Your Workplace Culture." *Forbes*, Forbes Magazine, 21 Nov. 2016, www.forbes.com/sites/amymorin/2016/11/20/how-an-authentic-thank-you-can-change-your-workplace-culture/.

Mutabaruka, Moses. "Leadership 101 - Lessons from Dr. Myles Munroe." *TAP Magazine*, TAP Magazine, 16 Apr. 2016, www.tapmagonline.com/tap/leadership-lessons-from-dr-myles-munroe.

Nee, Watchman. *Spiritual Authority.* Christian Fellowship Publishers, 1972. Page 66

Obama, Michelle. "Becoming." *Becoming*, by Michelle Obama, Viking, an Imprint of Penguin Books, 2018.

Prime, Jeanine and Elizabeth R. Salib. "Inclusive Leadership: The View of Six Countries." New York: Catalyst, 2014.

Seago, Jane. "Hubris: Leadership's Fatal Flaw." Toastmaster Magazine. July 2019 Page 28.

Spacey, John. "18 Examples of Influence." Simplicable, February 27 2016. simplicable.com/new/influence.

Stone, A. Gregory, et al. "Transformational versus Servant Leadership: a Difference in Leader Focus." *Leadership & Organization Development Journal*, vol. 25, no. 4, 2004, pp. 349–361., doi:10.1108/01437730410538671.

The Christian Worker (Colossians 3:22-4:1) | Bible.org. https://bible.org/seriespage/15-christian-worker-colossians-322-41

The Holy Bible: King James Version. T. Nelson, 1993.

"The Marks of a Spiritual Leader." *Desiring God*, 9 July 2019, www.desiringgod.org/articles/the-marks-of-a-spiritual-leader.

Trapp, Roger. "Why Leaders Need To Be Positive Thinkers." *Forbes.* Forbes Magazine, 04 Feb. 2014. Web. 12 July 2019

Yuen, Eunice Y, et al. "Repeated Stress Causes Cognitive Impairment by Suppressing Glutamate Receptor Expression and Function in Prefrontal Cortex." *Neuron*, U.S. National Library of Medicine, 8 Mar. 2012, www.ncbi.nlm.nih.gov/pmc/articles/PMC3302010/.

Udemy: Unshakable Confidence Title: What Makes a Leader by Daniel Goleman (Organizational Influence Processes, 229-241 2003 (Google Scholar)

https://www.biblegateway.com

https://www.google/amp/s/www.otquestions.org/amp/Bible-complaining.html

https://www.calvaryeauclaire.org/gods-model-for-servant-leadership/ retrieved 8-24-18. August 27, 2018

http://likeateam.com/9-characteristics-of-jesus-as-a-servant/

https://www.paulcarl.com/book-notes/
dale-carnegie-29-principles-win-friends-influence-people)

http://examples.yourdictionary.com/examples-of-core-values.html

https://www.abc.net.au/radionational/programs/allinthemind/
the-scientificevidence-for-positive-thinking/6553614

GLOSSARY

acronym - an abbreviation formed from the initial letters of other words and pronounced as a word

adroit - clever or skillful in using the hands or mind.

bottom-up leadership - an act of influence by someone other than the organizational leader, such as when an employee convinces the leader or management to adopt their ideas.

core values - the fundamental beliefs of a person or organization. These principles dictate behavior and can help people define the difference between right and wrong.

group-think - the practice of thinking or making decisions as a group in a way that discourages creativity or individual responsibility.

mnemonic - a device such as a pattern of letters, ideas, or associations that assists in remembering something.

GROW model - a simple method for goal setting and problem solving.

Hubris - excessive pride, a disastrous personal flaw that blinded human judgement

reframing - a technique used in <u>therapy</u> and by coaches to help others create a different way of looking at a situation, person, or relationship by changing its meaning. It can be referred to as cognitive reframing https://www.verywellmind.com/reframing-defined-2610419

self-Actualization - the realization or fulfillment of one's talents and potentialities, especially considered as a drive or need present in everyone.

SMART GOALS - to create structure and trackability in accomplishing your goals. SMART is the mnemonic acronym for Specific, Measurable, Attainable, Relevant and Time-based. These goals help one set specific objectives, measurable milestones, attainable timelines and outcome intervals that can be reasonably be made, relevant to your situation/business and be time-based, having an anticipated attainment date set.

social intelligence - the capacity to effectively negotiate complex social relationships and environments. https://educalingo.com/en/dic-en/social-intelligence

status quo means keeping the existing, particularly as it relates to social or political issues the way they presently are.

top-down leadership - used by a **leader** who wants as much control over the decision-making process as possible.

The practices identified in Leading God's Way will foster a unified culture of trust and a willingness to move toward common goals. Dr. Howard hopes that this book will stimulate conversations and cause leadership training programs to include more emphasis on this perspective. She is confident that cultivating coaching leaders in any workplace will create stronger communities of competent, confident workers. If you are interested in transformative leadership, try Leading God's Way.

Printed in the United States
By Bookmasters